FACING THE
MOUNTAINS

MY TESTIMONY

BY SHIRKYRIA GRAY

PROFESSIONAL PUBLISHING MEETS POWERFUL PROMOTION

A wholly owned subsidary of TBN

Facing the Mountains: My Testimony

Trilogy Christian Publishers A Wholly Owned Subsidiary of Trinity Broadcasting Network

2442 Michelle Drive Tustin, CA 92780

Manufactured in the United States of America

10 9 8 7 6 5 4 3 2 1

Library of Congress Cataloging-in-Publication Data is available.

ISBN: 978-1-63769-304-9

E-ISBN: 978-1-63769-305-6

Dedicated in loving memory of my
Daddy Meaddill.

Your life was a blessing, and you
will be missed beyond measure.

Acknowledgments

I give God honor and praise for all He has done. I thank Him for the many miracles that He did so that my dad would receive the care he needed. I would not have made it through the battles if it was not for God. I thank Him for never leaving me and giving me strength to endure the climb up the mountains. Joshua 1:9 says, "Be strong and of good courage; don't be afraid, nor be dismayed, for the Lord your God is with you wherever you go." I thank Him for helping me write this book. All glory belongs to God. My desire for this book is to be a blessing to not only caregivers but people that are going through difficult times and feel alone. I am a living witness of God's existence.

I want to thank my family that helped care for my dad in any way. A very special thank you to my husband Don, who was with me every step of the way and loved my dad unconditionally. Another special thank you to my uncle Kenneth and his wife Marilyn; they endured many hardships, but kept the faith, supported, cared for, and loved my dad so much. I would like to acknowledge my aunt Caroline and thank her for her love and support for my dad. My cousins Stephanie and Pat for the love and prayers as well as encouragement. Thank you to my mom Shironica, my sister Shirkydra and my granny Shirley for supporting me and inspiring me to finish the book. Thank you to Sis Donna and Lashun for their encouragement and prayers. Thank you to my in-laws Donald and Jacquelyn, for helping us maneuver through some murky waters. Thank you to former supervisors at Maximus for your support and understanding. Thanks to all the care staff that loved and cared for my dad at Autumn Leaves Memory Care, The Adult Day Care, Deborah at Home Health, the Nursing Homes in Oklahoma City, Enid, and Medford Oklahoma, Former President Obama, Social Security Regional Office, our lawyer Jerry and his team, the judge at the family court, Shanna at Adult Protective Services, Humanity hospice team, Eternal Rest and Lanman funeral home, grief counselor, and the Oklahoma Alzheimer's Association. Thank you, thank you!

If you would like to support, donate, or know of a caregiver that would benefit from S.Y.G, please reach out to us at:

www.sendingyougifts.org

https://www.facebook.com/sygsendingyougifts

Table of Contents

Introduction

My name is Shirkyria, and I am the founder of S.Y.G (Sending You Gifts) Through Thoughts of Love. I am a military wife and a mother of three beautiful children that I love with all my heart. I am a living testimony! I truly believe in miracles because I am a miracle. My story as a caregiver is a story that is wrapped in blood, sweat, tears, depression, loneliness, strength, and overall *faith*! In this book, I will share with you my journey as a caregiver for my father. It was not an easy or happy experience, but one in which I learned how to navigate through situations that seemed virtually impossible. I had no idea of what loomed ahead of me, and I was not prepared, but God knew what I needed and ensured that I received it at just the right time. Through this book, you will read about my brokenness, my confusion, the times that I wanted to give in, and how God took all of that and still used me. Caregivers need a lot of support, and I say *amen* to that! As a caregiver, I want to share my story to help others going through similar situations that feel as though this journey is too hard. If you are currently a caregiver or foresee yourself being a caregiver, I want you to know that you are not alone. It takes faith, patience, understanding, and unconditional love to take care of someone that may not end up knowing who you are. You may be caring for a parent, close relative, family member, or friend while facing and overcoming mountains. You may feel like you hit rock bottom or unappreciated, tired, overwhelmed, and frustrated.

I want you to know that I am going to be real and transparent. There were hills, valleys, and cliffs with sheer dropoffs, and at times I didn't hear or see God but knew He was with me to see that I made it through.

I thought that after my dad had transitioned from this life to the next, things would get better, but my battle continued as my health, life, and emotions took a turn for the worse. God picked me up from the darkest and loneliest of places and brought me back into the light of life, allowing me to share my story. Standing on the precipice of the mountain, I now see that God had a plan the entire time. However, I could not see over the mountain until He elevated me above the shallows and shadows, giving me a deeper understanding of how important it is to activate your faith. During these battles, faith was my weapon of choice because without faith, I was vulnerable to the attacks of the enemy. I now understand that no matter how big the problem is that God is much bigger. Luke 1:37 states that with God, nothing (*nothing*) shall be impossible.

INTRODUCTION

I encourage you to remain faithful and know that the same God that brought me through is going to bring you through as well! Allow God to be your source of strength and realize that you are stronger than you can possibly imagine.

Chapter 1

My Dad

Prior to being diagnosed with Alzheimer's, my father was known for his personality. He loved to joke and make people laugh; he would have you laughing so hard tears would fall, and bellies would ache. His presence would lift the darkness from any room, and his jubilant behavior was very contagious. My dad was born in the small town of Trumbull, Texas. Growing up, he was known for how well he played baseball. However, as an adult, his eyesight began to fade, and he became legally blind. His eyesight hindered him in many ways. I remember him telling me that he wanted to play professional baseball but could not pursue it due to his eyesight. Later, when he fell ill, I had to make a tough decision and place him into healthcare, and I would decorate his room with baseball memories hoping it would give him something to hold onto. His face lit up the day he found out that his grandsons started playing baseball; it was as if his legacy could continue vicariously through his grandkids, and that thought made him happy. He loved his family as he was considered a favorite uncle amongst many nieces and nephews. He also loved his brothers and sister. However, he had a very special relationship with his cousin, whom he looked at as a brother. The two lived together for many, many years until my dad's health started to decline.

As a child, I did not live with my dad since my parents split up when I was a baby. I lived with my mom but would visit my dad on weekends, some holidays, and part of the summers. I loved visiting my dad. When I was a little girl, my dad would always dress me up so pretty and loved doing my hair with matching hair bows. He had me floating around town like a princess. I was truly the definition of a daddy's girl. He spoiled me; I never left my dad's house empty-handed. One Christmas, when I was about ten years old, my dad bought me my first mountain bike. It was black and pink, and I rode that bike until the wheels fell off. When I was in the sixth grade, I was really struggling with math, and one of my friends was really good with math, so my dad made a deal with her that if she tutored me and I brought my math grade up, he would take us both shopping. That was some motivation! When my next report card came out, my math grade improved, and he did exactly what he said. Oh, it felt like Christmas! He bought us so many clothes and my friend and I were so excited. My dad loved to surprise me all the time. He loved buying me jewelry. I learned early how it felt to get jewelry because that is what my dad did for me. It felt wonderful to be treated like a queen, and my father laid the foundation for what I should expect out of a man. For example, when I was in high school, one day after school, I was walking outside of the school getting ready to go home when I spotted my dad in the front of the school waiting for me with a teddy bear in hand. The bear was holding a box, and inside was a beautiful ring. First of all, I was just happy to see my dad, but the fact that he surprised me with such a beautiful gift from the heart really made my day. He constantly went out of his way to put a smile on my face every chance he got. I will never forget on my twelfth birthday, he threw me a birthday party at my uncle's house located in Ferris, Texas, and I tell y'all, my dad bought me the biggest birthday cake. I mean, it was huge and was every bit of two full sheets of cake with Minnie Mouse on it. I had so much fun. That's a birthday party I will never forget. He cherished my brother and me. He was the type of man that put others before himself and extended his hand out to those in need time and time again, and for that, he was my hero and still is. I admired my dad so much because although he was disabled, he was very much independent and did not let his disabilities limit his love for life. Since he couldn't drive due to his eyesight, we would always catch the bus to wherever we had to go. Oftentimes family and friends would lend him a ride if he needed to go anywhere, but he would always seem to find his way around.

He worked at Borden Dairy company for over twenty

years. I remember him bringing home different flavors of juices! Every time I visited him, he had crates of juices, tea, and milk. Even as an adult, when we would visit family in Texas, he would make sure that me, my husband, and his grandkids had crates of juices. He knew the orange flavor was my favorite, so that was always on the list. Even though my dad had issues with his sight, he was still physically able to work with some limitations. He never allowed his eyesight to cripple his style or keep him from living his best life. Let me tell you a funny story... In 2008, we were stationed at Hill AFB in Utah, and my husband was deployed to Iraq, our oldest son was two, and our youngest was about six months old. My dad kept talking about flying to Utah to see us. At first, I didn't take him seriously because he had never traveled outside of Texas. He didn't want to fly alone, so he brought his son along with him. During his stay in Utah, the base put on an event for the deployed members' spouses. It was a retreat getaway to the mountains; we stayed in a nice condo that was paid for by the Air Force. My dad had never even seen real mountains before, and while we were there, they had activities set up for us to do, and one of the activities was canoeing. My dad really wanted to do the canoeing, but I was scared because I don't know how to swim. However, I decided to go because I knew it meant a lot to him. So we got into a canoe with another father and two daughters; the other father was doing the rowing when all of a sudden we realized that we had gone out too far. My anxiety started to rise once I saw how far away from the shore. My dad could see the terrifying look on my face, and he started chuckling. I was anxious to get out of the boat. We turned around and headed back towards the shore, but when we got close, I was out of that boat! I was standing in two feet of water while the other father was still trying to park the boat, and my dad was laughing so hard because I didn't even give him a chance to stop the boat. He made a joke about me being like Jesus trying to walk on water. He told that story to everybody and got a good laugh out of it for years to come.

I can brag on my dad all day. Of course, no one is perfect, and like any other family, we had our own issues, but I loved my dad for who he was and for everything he had done for me. He was not just a great dad; he was loved by family and so many people. There was never a dull moment with him. He went above and beyond for his kids and grandkids when he was able. Although it got tough in the end, he will forever be remembered for his magnificent sense of humor, unconditional love, and for the man he was to his family and friends. His compassion for others enabled him to make a huge impact on people's lives. When you needed him, he was always there, hands down! That was the man that I want you to know as you begin this journey with me.

Chapter 2

The Beginning

Okay, now that you know a little bit about my dad and how my child and teenage years went with him, let's fast forward in time. After high school, my life changed pretty quickly, and I decided to get married. My husband had just entered the Air Force, and we got stationed at Hill Air Force Base in Utah, where we started our family and had three beautiful kids. We were there for about eight years and finally got orders to Misawa, Japan. I did not know what to expect since I had never left the US before. I would never have thought that little ol' me would find her way over the Pacific Ocean *ever*. We were both very excited to have an opportunity to travel abroad and see the world. My experience living in northern Japan for three years was amazing. My family and I met some amazing people and experienced a culture that opened our eyes as well as our hearts.

While in Japan, I had found my flow in my life. I started getting on track to losing weight; I became a Zumba instructor. I was finding myself because I had struggled with losing weight after having kids. I was in a place that allowed me to focus on bettering myself and making new friends.

We loved Japan. It was a great experience, but we were missing our family back home, and we wanted to be closer to Texas so that we could spend more time with family. God showed us favor, and in 2014, my husband received orders to Tinker Air Force base located in Oklahoma. We were so excited, and so was the family, that we would finally be a little closer to home.

Once we touched down back in the United States, we decided to make a pit stop to Texas for just a few days to visit with our family before heading to Oklahoma. During this transition is where things started to get real for me. When we arrived in Dallas, I found out that my father was about to be evicted from his apartment, which was a shock because he always paid his bills on time.

My dad was very disciplined when it came to paying bills on time and saving money, so this was an immediate red flag for me. When I arrived at his apartment, I asked about the eviction, and he was confused as if he had no idea. When I questioned my dad about the unpaid rent, he thought he had made his payments when in reality, he simply couldn't remember the due dates.

I had not seen my dad in a while, and I didn't expect that the next time I visited him that he would be kicked out of his place of living. The apartments he stayed in had charged him with late fees along with court fees. He was summed to attend court due to unpaid rent.

I decided to visit the front office of the apartments and have a conversation with the office manager. The manager explained to me that she knew something was wrong with my dad when he came into the office to pay rent with cash even though he knew they only accepted money orders or check. The manager also said that when she told him they couldn't accept cash, he came back the very next day to pay his rent with cash again, and she had to tell him again that they couldn't accept cash for rent payment. She stated that my dad never came back to pay his rent, which led to the eviction. We decided to stay in Dallas for a few more days. The day before, my dad had to go to court; my husband, kids, and I stayed the night at his apartment. Attending court was uncomfortable because I just couldn't wrap my head around him ever being in this position. The judge ordered him to pay rent, fees, and to move out of the apartment. The look on his face was that of confusion and frustration, which just broke my heart. There was so much going on with him and his finances that it did not sit right me. As we left the courthouse, I needed to let my dad know that we were heading to Oklahoma to get settled and that once evicted, he would have to stay with his brother and sister for a little bit until he got back on his feet. His life had taken a complete 180-degree turn for the worse, and this was just the beginning.

I got in the car, and tears were just flowing. I did not know how to process what he was going through. Within a week of searching, we found a rent home in South West Oklahoma City. I received a phone call from a longtime friend of my dad's letting me know that she was visiting her sister in Norman, Oklahoma, which was about twenty minutes away from me. She said that she wanted to see me and asked if I would meet her at a Walmart. As I walked inside of Walmart, I called her to let her know that I was waiting. I walked outside to meet her, and out of nowhere, I see my *dad!* Yes, I was happy to see him, but at the same time, I was so confused. I had no idea that he was planning to come to Oklahoma. Apparently, he talked her into taking him to Oklahoma and did not inform anyone. I notified his siblings that he was safe and in Oklahoma with me. I had to drive my dad back to Texas a few days later because he had a scheduled doctor's appointment. A couple of days after taking him back, I received a phone call that a neurologist doctor had evaluated my dad and, based on the evaluation, diagnosed him with early-onset dementia. Dementia is a group of symptoms that affect your memory and behavior. Dementia is most commonly found in older adults, but it can also affect people under the age of sixty-five, and my dad was only fifty-three. He moved out of his apartment and, for the time being, lived back and forth between his brother and sister.

When we finally got settled in Oklahoma City, God blessed me with a job. I was hired at a company that dealt with Sooner Care which is Medicaid for the state of Oklahoma. Little did I know that this job was preparing me with the tools and knowledge I would need for battle later on down the road. I had weekends off and used some of them to go home since Oklahoma City was only a little over a three-hour drive to Dallas. During the week, I would always call to check on him, and the family would keep me posted on any behavior changes.

I started to condemn myself for not being able to do enough. His behavior had become more difficult to handle. His brother and sister did the best that they could to keep him in a normal and stable environment, but the day came to where it was time for him to move with me to Oklahoma. The sad truth is that when someone suffers from this illness, home is not the safest place for them, and I had to learn that the hard way.

The day we had to pick up my dad from Texas, it was late. My husband, kids, and I got up and left Oklahoma around midnight. We arrived in Texas around 2:00 a.m. and picked him up from my uncle's house. On the way back to Oklahoma, my dad didn't say much. We stopped to get some gas, and my dad says, "I am sorry that I keep taking ya'll through this." My husband responded, "It's okay man, we got you and will make sure to get you the help you need." My dad said, "I don't know what's wrong with me, but I'm going to fight this." At this point, I was at the base of the mountain, looking up and not knowing where the top of it ended. The long drive was draining, and on top of that, I had to be at work in the next few hours.

When I arrived at work, I didn't know how I was going to tell my boss that I may have to quit my job. I spoke with my supervisor and explained my unforeseen situation. I could sense that my supervisor understood that my hands were tied because he could tell by the frustration and emotion radiating from the conversation. However, my boss was also a social worker and was such a big help. He gave me resources to start with and allowed me to take a few days off to get things lined up. This was the point where I started to climb the mountain alone. I can't stress how important it is to ensure that your loved one has their legal affairs in order before they decline. There were many times that I relied upon my power of attorney and guardianship to help me maneuver through many situations. I was so glad that we had hired an elder law attorney early on that was extremely knowledgeable and helped us through the process, and my father really liked him.

While my dad was staying in our home, we would do things with him to take his mind off the stress and emotions that he was dealing with. We spent a lot of family time together, and we did different activities. My dad would make comments saying how he wished he could hit the streets and drive. One day we took him to this indoor race cart track, and he had the absolute time of his life racing me and his grandkids.

I was reaching out to different experts daily due to rapid behavioral changes and was advised to take him to the doctor for further evaluation. We took him to an inpatient behavioral medicine facility so they could adjust his medications to balance him out. While he was there, I would visit him almost every day. It was so hard to see him in a place like that.

After a two-week evaluation period, the doctor, facility social worker, and care staff sat down with me and my husband and told us that they initially thought he was at the beginning stage of dementia, but after further evaluation, he was deemed in the advanced stages of dementia. The type of dementia he had was Alzheimer's. The doctor informed me that from their experience, patients that have advanced early-onset dementia pass away quicker, typically within two or three years. I had a hard time processing this information; my heart was hurting for my dad. The social worker forewarned me and advised that whatever my dad said to me in a mean way, if he came off aggressive or called me names, to try not to take it personally. She needed me to understand and be prepared. She stated for me to keep in mind it wasn't my dad; it was the disease. As for his memory, the way she described it was like a Jigsaw puzzle. She said that the puzzle was never completed because one day, some pieces would be there, and the next day those pieces could be gone, and new pieces would be down. However, the days of the complete picture being shown were over. This is what drove his frustration because he was trying to figure things out, but all the pieces were not there for him to make sense of it. The worst part of the conversation was when the doctor told me that there would come a time when my father will not remember me. *What!* This was my dad! How could he not remember me, his own daughter? Everything that we had experienced was going to eventually be forgotten. This news stung badly! I was not prepared or ready to hear anything like this. It didn't seem fair that there are people that can live with dementia for years or even decades, but my dad gets a two-to-three-year death diagnosis. This became almost too much to bear. However, my heart absolutely went to my dad, who was so determined to fight through this. This was the point where it was important to face the mountain together and tether ourselves to one another to prevent gravity from pulling us back down to earth. We started our accent together.

Chapter 3

The Mountain In Front Of Me

While my dad was still admitted into the behavioral facility, the doctor and the social worker highly advised me to find a nursing home placement for him *ASAP*. Since I had three younger children in the home, the doctor deemed it unsafe to have my dad in my residence. When they told me this, I was appalled. In my mind, I was thinking to myself like, "this is my dad; he wouldn't hurt my kids, nor me," but on the other hand, I didn't realize the lack of awareness that came with aggressive Alzheimer's disease. Having to accept this fact was very hard for me, and it backed me up into a corner. I didn't want to deliver this news to my dad because I knew that it would break his heart.

After meeting with the doctor, we met back with the attorney and explained to him what the doctor told us. I thought I had already got bad news, but we got introduced to another problem. Remember I shared with you how prior to my dad being diagnosed with dementia, he had problems with his eyesight? My dad had basically been blind since I was a little girl, so he was able to receive social security disability while having a part-time job. Since he was receiving social security disability, he could not work more than a certain amount of hours during the week. We explained to the lawyer that social security had stopped giving him disability checks years ago due to him working too many hours at his job.

Hold on; this was not it. Due to him working all those extra hours while still receiving benefits, he owed social security a large overpayment debt. With this hanging over our heads, the lawyer knew that that was going to be a battle attempting to apply for social security again for my dad's disability since he now owed social security debt. My dad didn't have many assets; he didn't own a home or any businesses. He had very little savings that he had in a CD, and he also had 4o1k, that's it. The lawyer explained to me with applying for Medicaid, he can't have over a certain amount. So, we did a spend-down plan that covered expenses that would help my dad and provide for his needs. The lawyer also suggested to buy a cheap car for my dad in case I needed to take him to appointments or any other obligations that required travel. My dad was close to being discharged from the behavioral facility, so I needed to find him a nice facility quick to stay in for at least a month while the lawyer and I started the Medicaid application process, and it was basically because he didn't have enough money to cover for an out-of-pocket memory care/assisted living facility. This also gave me time to look at nursing homes.

Even though my dad couldn't work at his previous job anymore, he was entitled to receive short-term disability through the job because he worked at Borden's for so long. Mind you; we were still waiting on social security to respond. So, I was relieved that he would receive some sort of consistent income now to help pay for whatever he needed, but of course, things could not go smoothly. We came across another hump in the road. My dad's healthcare coverage through Borden's had expired. I screamed! *Ugh!* Why couldn't this just wait until he was approved for long-term care Medicaid? Since he was terminated from Borden's, he was no longer eligible to receive the group health care insurance. Meaning I had to find health care insurance until the state of Oklahoma Medicaid approved him. The way health care cost had gone up, I knew his premiums were going to be high. However, I was grateful that he had some income to help cover his premium so that I could still get his medicine and pay for his doctor's visits. If I give you any type of advice, it is so crucial to ensure your loved one has the proper insurance.

My dad had a life insurance policy through the previous employer, and I was told that in order for him not to lose the policy through the company, I would need to send them updated medical records consistently about his condition. I would also have to notify them of his location, and that involved a lot of paperwork overtime. Keeping this paperwork in order was very important. Eventually, I had to buy another file cabinet just to keep things organized. Listen, it is very important that when you are doing a spend-down, keep all your documents and receipts because you will need to do an annual financial report on everything that was spent and provide it to the courts.

There was so much that needed to be done; I had to talk to my boss again because my time was consumed with getting my father squared away. I needed more time off to find a facility for my dad. Initially, I was stressed out because I had the feeling that I was going to lose my job at this point. I needed more than a few more days off, more like two-three weeks, but I was willing to sacrifice my job to take care of these things for my dad. This was hard for me to deal with because I did not want my husband trying to maintain the household on his own, although he has always been supportive through the process. I remember calling my boss and updating him on my dad's situation. I was expecting him to say, "I'm sorry I can't give you any more time off. I would have to let you go." To my surprise, that was not what he said! My supervisor and boss suggested that I apply for a six-week leave of absence due to medical circumstances with a family member. It was no guarantee that it would get approved, but at this time, anything was worth a shot. After this amazing surprise, I called the company my job was contracted with. The person I was assigned to sent me all the leave paperwork for me and the doctor to fill out. This was another miracle that only God was able to work out for me.

While I was busy with paperwork and taking care of business, I still was ensuring the safety of my father was a priority; during this time, he was still in the behavioral facility. I called every day at least four-five times to check on him, and most days, the nurses would tell me that he was doing and eating really well. I was glad to hear that he was doing better. My dad loved to eat! Whatever was put in front of him, he would eat it. He was not picky at all. When it came time to eat, he did not play! His favorite restaurant was a local buffet, and he would eat until he started sweating. It would be so funny.

My heart melted because, during the visits, the nurses would tell me that he bragged and talked about how much he missed his grandkids. He could not see them because this was a secured location, and kids were not allowed in the area for safety reasons. However, for one of the visits, the doctor made an exception. Although it was for a short period of time, the doctor took us to a room where it was just my dad, me, my husband, and our children. When I say that this made his day, *y'all,* this made his day. He smiled from ear to ear, and he was so happy to see us. He played and played with his grandkids. I enjoyed seeing him happy. I explained to the doctor that I needed some paperwork to be filled out for my job so that I could take more time off to find placement for my dad, and she helped with that. After a few days of submitting my leave paperwork, it was approved for six weeks. God gave me favor because I strongly felt that I was going to lose my job.

I was so grateful and relieved at the same time. God came through in our time of need. God supplied. God protected. God directed. God has the last say so on all decisions! "Cast your burden on the Lord and he shall sustain you; He shall never permit the righteous to be moved" (Psalm 55:22).

My dad still had belongings in storage from his apartment in Texas, like his bedroom furniture, clothes, and shoes. Trying to get his belongings situated was starting to become a burden. It was exhausting! Between the back and forth from Oklahoma to Texas, I was literally going one hundred miles an hour. I was constantly moving; I had no time to slow down. I was so thankful to have my husband by my side! He is my biggest supporter! Being in the military is a demanding job, and he has a very hectic schedule, yet, he made the time to take off work and support me and my father's process. I felt so blessed to have a caring and supportive husband.

Once we got everything situated, it gave me time to get back on track here in Oklahoma. My husband and I started the journey by visiting memory care facilities. The ones we visited were very upscale, nice, and clean, but I was blown away by the monthly cost. The cost was starting at $6,000 a *month*. I thought to myself, *how can people afford this? Are these places just for rich people? Why won't these places accept state payment?* Some actually go as far as selling their homes just to be able to afford living in a memory care facility.

I came across one that really stood out to me. The outside and inside looked fairly new; it was beautiful and not too big. The big plus was that it was only five minutes from my house. As soon as we walked in, I explained why I was there to the sales director, who was so nice and welcoming, and we had a long interesting conversation. I learned that she was also dealing with a family member that had dementia. We talked about how sad it is that the state would not cover the costs for someone with dementia to live in a memory care facility. We did not understand how the state could pay for a nursing home, which is about the same price.

This place really gave me the warm and fuzzy feeling that I needed, but I was still trying to deal with the thought of having to send my dad here. After we talked, I was given a tour around the facility. I enjoyed seeing that the residents had some form of independence. The rooms were spacious. In the room, they had their own bathroom, they had an elegant dining room, and served high-quality food. They also had a back patio that was surrounded by a locked gate where residents could go out and sit on their own. This place caught my attention because though it was a memory care, it gave the residents the feeling of having their own apartment with around-the-clock care. It had grown on me so much that it irked me that my dad could only afford to stay for a month. This *sucked* big time! This place was perfect in my eyes, and it would only take me five minutes to get to him. This was everything he needed.

Moving him from his home was so stressful and heart-breaking; I just knew that he would want to feel and be in his own space after being independent the majority of his life. I wanted him to feel as comfortable as possible. Once all the paperwork and care plan was in place, the sales director stated that we could move my dad's things in.

As you can tell, it was a process getting my dad admitted into the memory care facility. I called the social worker at the behavioral facility and told her where he was moving to. Now we were on a mission to getting his room set up, I felt overwhelmed, but I was determined to take care of business for my dad. He was my responsibility.

A couple of my husband's coworkers were nice enough to help us move his bedroom furniture to his room. While they were moving the big furniture, I was organizing his clothes, shoes and hanging up family pictures along with wall décor. I wanted his room to be nice and homey. When I tell you we spent all day and most of the night getting his room together, it took a lot of work. We were so exhausted it wasn't even funny. I didn't care, though, because I wanted my dad's room to be perfect. Once I was satisfied, I knew that when my dad saw his room, he would be ecstatic. My dad was discharged from the behavioral facility the following day. We went out to eat at his favorite local buffet. He was in good spirits laughing and joking. Even though he seemed like himself, I could tell that a part of my dad was different; he just wasn't the same. While we were eating, I had to put on that mask to hide my concern to enjoy this moment with him.

I knew that this was just the beginning of the process and that the journey was nowhere near being stabilized. The thought of having to move my dad again after a month had already started to stress me out. I didn't want to even think about the thought of putting my dad in a nursing home. I didn't want to go looking at any nursing homes because it just put me down. Just like you, I had so many "Why, God?" moments. I cried out to God on multiple occasions asking, "Why did this disease have to come upon my dad? Why was this happening to him? Lord, this is too much to carry." I found myself getting angry with God, angry at the disease, and angry at those around me. This was so overwhelming, and we were still in the beginning stages. However, I continued to maintain my strength.

After eating, we finally made it to the memory care facility. When we walked in, the care staff and the directors all greeted and welcomed my dad. He smiled and laughed with them. In my head, I was like, *"Whoo!* So far so good." As we were escorted back to his room, my nerves got bad fast because I didn't know how he was going to respond. When we walked into his room, to my surprise, he loved his room. He recognized his bed and dresser and fell in love with his recliner. Seeing him happy and excited was a relief for me. I was happy seeing that my dad was pleased. I told y'all that my dad *loved* to eat, so he was that much happier when we told him about the fine dining and that he would be served a good breakfast, lunch, and dinner with snacks in between. Boy, his expression was priceless—hahahaha. He said *"Fo-*

real!" and started laughing.

Once we got him relaxed and comfortable, the director came to my dad's room to make sure everything was good. They immediately made him feel at home, and they were genuinely nice to him. Seeing the treatment that he was getting had me thinking like, *Maannn, why can't my dad just stay here?* This was the perfect place for him. We showed my dad where everything was in his room. We showed him how to call the nurses when he needed help, even in the bathroom. He did not have one complaint; he accepted it immediately. Before we departed, I had conversations with the nurses that were assigned to my dad to make sure they knew his care plan. I let him know that I would be calling and visiting him quite often. I wanted to make sure that he knew that I was right down the street. My dad was good to go, and we left feeling relieved that he would be okay.

Chapter 4

Home Away From Home— The Ascent

I visited my dad basically every day for the month that he was at the memory care facility. I knew that moving him out of Texas was out of his comfort zone, so I wanted to be sure that he felt my love every day. He needed to know that I wasn't far away. I didn't want him to get to the point of thinking that when I left, I was never coming back.

One visit with him, I knocked on the door a few times saying "Daddy," but, at first, he didn't answer. After a few more knocks and me calling his name at the door, he finally opened the door. I started to panic, but from the looks of things, he had obviously been sleeping. I entered his room, and I noticed that his room was a mess. He had clothes everywhere, and I could smell that he had urinated in the bed. It melted my heart because the look on my dad's face showed me that he was confused. I was still mad, though! I went and got the nurses and started asking them a load of questions. I asked them about their knowledge concerning his care plan. The nurses on that shift seemed clueless; they didn't know anything about his care plan. I was not a happy daughter. I had to explain to them his daily needs, such as assisting with getting dressed. I explained the urgency of reminding him would help him. I was frustrated how this information was not passed down to them. I didn't want my dad just sitting in his room all day. I was so angry, and they saw it all over my face. After my rant with the nurses, I stayed to clean my dad's room and to put everything back in order. While I was cleaning his room, the nurses cleaned his bathroom and brought him some snacks. Once I saw that my dad was good, I left and went home.

The very next day, I called the director and expressed my concern. She assured me that that incident would not happen again and that they would make sure that all the nurses and CNA's knew of his care plan. After that, I didn't have any more issues; the staff stayed on top of things. Everyone was finally on the same page with his care plan.

Although I was getting things situated at the memory care facility, I still had another mission to accomplish: finding a nursing home. I had a list of nursing homes from the social worker at the behavioral medicine facility and the lawyer. My lawyer wanted me to notify them once I had found a nursing home so that they could send the necessary paper-work over to them. The lawyer notified me about how most nursing homes would still admit him under pending Medicaid since we were still waiting on the approval for long-term care. I never thought of putting my dad in a nursing home; this was hard to even consider. The very first nursing home I toured was not good. As soon as I walked in, my first thought was that there was no way that I was placing my dad in a nursing home. *I can't do this! No way!* However, the reality was that he couldn't stay in the memory care facility and that alone got under my skin. Most of the nursing homes had a bad smell, and I couldn't stand it. The rooms were small and old. It would be a downgrade because he couldn't have his own room. He had no choice but to share a room. From the way I was feeling, I knew for a fact that my dad was not going to like this move. I knew that he would be angry with me about this.

Over the course of two to three weeks, I toured nearly thirty nursing homes. Some of them were decent, but they would not take him due to him still being young. A few of them were concerned with having a really young patient around much older patients. There were other decent nursing homes, but they were full. My time was winding down, and my stress level was rising. It got to a point where I would spend the whole day looking at nursing homes. It was painful, and I dreaded it.

Once I finished my search for the day touring nursing homes, we always stopped at the memory care to check on my dad. Most times, he was doing well. He was participating in the activities. The chef cooked the food from scratch, I mean, the food was fantastic! Which he loved. They had a barbershop which was neat, but when it came time for a haircut and beard trim, my husband would always take him to his barber. The staff really loved him. He was always cracking jokes with them and would make them laugh, and that would make their day. Some days I would sit and eat lunch with him, and other days I would sit and watch him do activities such as bowling and other games the residents played.

I loved how the memory care facility was so engaged with him and my family. He was always doing something; with having Alzheimer's, he needed stimulation. This gave me some relief. He needed to stay in a place like this. It's what he needed. The state was making this so hard. This was so unfair, and the more I thought about it, the angrier I got.

After a long search, it finally came down to the last two nursing homes on my list. Out of those two nursing homes, one of them was decent. The distance was not too bad. It was about twenty minutes from my home. I wanted him much closer, but at that point, I did not have many choices left.

I walked into the nursing home, and it smelled clean and looked clean. However, the thought of putting my dad in a nursing home still had my nerves bad. The administrator gave me and my husband a tour of the nursing home. I was kind of impressed. It didn't compare to the place he was at the time. They had a schedule of activities which was big for me so that my dad didn't get bored or wither away in his room. While taking the tour, I took the time to explain my dad's situation the best way I could to ensure she understood my dad's predicament. There were double rooms available; my dad would have to share with another male. I thought to myself, *I know for a fact my dad is not going to like this.* This wasn't the best, but I had to keep in mind that that nursing home was able to admit my dad under pending Medicaid instead of waiting for his long-term care to be approved before he could move in. The downside was there was still no decision with social security. The nursing home needs the vendor payment, which is paid through your social security, and the state pays the rest. It was an ongoing battle with social security about his overpayment. In the meantime, he was receiving disability income from his previous employer. They probably could not accept that as the vendor payment, which didn't make any sense to me. The administrator at the nursing home went to talk to the director regarding the situation. She came back to tell me that they would have to have a meeting to decide if they would accept the other disability payment. After she said that, I was done for the day. I didn't visit any more nursing homes.

On my way out of the nursing home, my mind was going one hundred miles an hour. I felt so heavy because I was weighed down with so many worries. I knew that I was running out of time. My dad had about one more week left in the memory care facility, and on top of that, he had no idea that he had to move again. When I tell you my nerves were bad, I was feeling sick to my stomach. I had so much on my mind. I needed a miracle from God at that moment.

The last few days in the memory care facility came, and I was a nervous wreck. My dad had to move out by the end of the month, which fell on a Saturday, so I needed an answer from the nursing home by Thursday, no later than Friday. While waiting to hear from the nursing home, I was still doing my normal visits with my dad. Boy! I tell you, it was hard keeping a smile on my face. On the inside, my stomach was in knots. I am grateful because although I was a mess, my dad was in a good place. I was held together because he was holding on, but it broke me down knowing that I had to break the news to him of moving. I was stressed out to the max, impatient. I couldn't sleep and couldn't handle everything that was being thrown my way. I felt like this nursing home was my last hope because I didn't have another plan. The waiting game was so intense. Wednesday came, and still, I had no phone call from the nursing home. I remember going into my room and breaking down in tears while crying out desperately to God, pleading for his help. I was panicking because I needed answers! I had no more patience at this point. My dad needed care, and that was all I could think about. My dad was depending on me. While others were sleeping like a baby, I was at the end of my rope. My husband was so worried about me; he had never seen me this stressed. He tried to encourage me that God would work it out and that everything would be fine, but I wasn't trying to hear that. I had no answer from anyone. I needed to know something right then! I couldn't control my emotions; it was too much for me.

After a sleepless couple of nights, I was on edge. I still had a little bit of hope that I would receive a phone call with the good news that my dad would be accepted. I felt the need to call the nursing home and give them a sense of urgency that I needed an answer right now. As soon as I called, the administrator let me know that they had just made a decision. They would accept my dad under pending Medicaid and use his current income as payment—*yes!* She also went to say that I could come and fill out the paperwork, and he would be able to move in the next day. When I tell you I felt relieved, God did a miracle! He heard my cries and answered my prayers right on time! I was so thankful and just praised God. I was still anxious about breaking the news to my dad. I knew that he was not going to be happy.

I informed the memory care directors that I had found a nursing home for my dad. They let me know that my dad and my family were welcomed anytime to visit and welcome to come to the family events. I appreciated that so much. I tried to explain to my dad the best way I could that he would be moving again. After I explained it in a way that he would understand, he just said, "Okay." I think he was just trying to accept it all as well because he didn't ask any questions.

Everything was in place with the paperwork, my dad was ready to roll, and we were finally set to move. We had a lot of stuff to move, so some of my husband's coworkers were nice enough again to help us move some of the things to the nursing home. The nursing home provided a bed, so we had to store his bedroom furniture in our garage. Although we had the help, we still had to put in work! Me, my kids, my husband, and some of his coworker spent hours back and forth from the memory care to the nursing home. My dad was still at the memory care while we were moving things out, so the staff kept him busy with activities. Even though he was sharing a room in the nursing home, I tried to set it up nice for him; the space was not that big and not luxurious. There was no mattress on the bed. It was basically a mat, so I knew this was not going to be comfortable for him. I went out and bought him a foam mattress to make his bed more comfortable.

We finally got his room together, and it was an exhausting day for all of us. This was the hard part of moving my dad once again. The guilt was so heavy. The staff at the memory care facility gave my dad hugs, we took pictures, and we said goodbyes. Though my dad was only there for a month, he was like family to them. It was a sad moment for us all.

We took my dad out to eat prior to taking him to the nursing home. All I could think about at the time was how my dad was going to feel once he saw his new place. Once we arrived at the nursing home. I pulled my dad to the side and tried to explain to him the best way I knew how about his new living accommodations.

When I tell you that he was not happy, the look on his face was not pleasing at all. I could tell that he was upset and confused. As I was talking to the administrator, I glanced over, and I see my dad sitting in a chair with an upset look on his face. The staff went over to introduce themselves to my dad to welcome him, which kind of snapped him out of being upset. We took him to his room, and I showed him where his things were and how we fixed up the room for him. We took him to the dining area and showed him where he would be eating and the activity schedule. We were really trying to cheer him up. I reassured him that we would still come to visit and that I would still come get him to take him out. I tried my best to put him at ease so that he didn't feel like he was going to be left there and that I was not coming back. Talking to him helped; I could tell that he was a little relieved.

We got him settled and decided to stay at the nursing home for a while to spend some extra time with him. I wanted to make sure that he was okay before we left to go home. Once I saw that he was feeling better, I let him know again that I would be calling and checking on him along with coming to see him. This is the important part about your journey with someone going through this: they need to know over and over again that they are not alone. There were times I could tell that he felt lonely, but I did my best to help him through that. All I could do was my best.

I am not telling you to put your loved one in a nursing home; it really depends on your situation. Many caregivers feel so guilty putting their loved one in a nursing home because it feels like your giving up on that person because you cannot take care of them full time 24/7, which is what they need. However, caregivers should not feel like they are giving up on their loved ones. They are just ensuring that their loved one is being provided for by a team of professionals as opposed to doing it all by yourself. There is only so much that you can do by yourself before it becomes too much of a burden and your health and affairs start to suffer because you exert so much energy on the other person. You have to take care of yourself too because if you get sick from not taking care of yourself, then who will take care of your loved one? Yes, it is a very, very hard decision! Trust me, I did not want to put my dad in the nursing home, but it was a difficult decision that had to be made. It literally made me sick to my stomach looking at nursing homes. During the ascent of the mountain, some bad weather rolled in, making it slippery to continue the climb, but God gave us a foot hole at the right time so that we could continue our climb.

Chapter 5

Battling with the State

Now that my dad was living in the nursing home, I expected things to coast out, but that was not the case. One of the biggest barriers throughout this whole process was the struggles I dealt with concerning the state. Battling with the state was so aggravating, irritating, and infuriating. This particular battle drained me mentally that you can imagine, but it doesn't just end when you overcome one hurdle. The race is a marathon, not a sprint.

As stated before, we got to a point where my dad was settled in, and things were going well for him. Things were beginning to calm down. I was able to go back to work and kind of get back into my routine while managing the care for my dad. More weeks had gone by, and there was still no decision with social security and Medicaid. Even though the nursing home agreed to take the income he currently had, for the time being, there was still the vendor payment to consider, which had to come from social security. We were still battling with the overpayment. It was a waiting game.

Sometimes I would get off work early just to stop by to check on him. I remember the times that I would just see him wandering the halls very confused, or he would be in his room sitting in his recliner. As a family, we would pick him up almost every Saturday just to get him out of that nursing home environment. We would bring him back to the house, and I would cook a nice meal. He always enjoyed my cooking and just being around family. Every time he was around his grandkids, it would bring a smile to his face. It would put him in a brighter mood. Family from Texas would come and visit him on some weekends, which also made him happy. I believe it made him feel at ease, knowing that his family didn't forget about him. Most Sundays, he attended church with us. When I could call to tell him that I was coming to get him, he would get ready, even if it was two different shoes on his feet with mixed match socks. He would be waiting by the front desk. He would get so happy to get in the car and even more excited when he heard my kids say, "Hey, Paw Paw!"

Most of the time, when I took him back to the nursing home, I would notice things in his room were out of order or missing. I got upset with the nursing home because things were not as they needed to be for my dad. I always made sure that my dad had all the toiletries he needed: toothbrush, toothpaste, mouth wash, deodorant, shaving cream, body wash, shampoo, etc. I put them all in a clear tote container and etched his name on them. Eventually, I got frustrated.

The toiletries weren't my only issue, sad to say. I was also upset because I could tell that the nursing home staff wasn't making sure that my dad was brushing his teeth. They knew that he needed to be reminded of things, but they failed to do so. It took everything in me not to blow up!

I would basically have to rebuy what he needed. I got to a point where I just wrote my dad's name on his clothes, so the nursing home wouldn't lose his clothes, but that didn't do any good because some of his clothes still came up missing. I finally told the nursing home that I would wash his clothes. Dad didn't have much closet space, so I organized it in a way where it would be easy for him to find things, but most of the time, I'd visit him; his stuff would be out of order still. I wasn't sure if it was my dad or the nurses being negligent. It may have been a combination of both. Between ensuring he had what he needed, keeping the nurses involved with his daily routine, and taking care of his clothes and closet, I was exhausted physically. The state and the nursing home were just showing me how my father was not their main priority, which made me feel even more alone.

In the midst of the state and the nursing home adding more stress on my plate, my dad was declining more drastically. One Sunday before church, I had sensed that his mood was different. He did not seem happy and was irritated about something. I understood that having this disease would change his moods, but the extreme of the swings was always iffy. About halfway through church service, my dad began fidgeting and pulling on his coat zippers and rocking back and forth. I asked him to be still, and he got irritated and said something under his breath. To be honest, my feelings got in the way, and I got upset at him. The look on his face told me how he felt instantly! He was upset with me. I immediately started thinking to myself that my dad was embarrassing me with his moody behavior. One of the church members, which happened to be a close friend of mine, was trying to get my dad to calm down. It got to a point where my husband had to take my dad outside to get him to calm down. Fresh air worked. When my dad came back inside, he was calm, and his attitude had completely changed. He was over it, but I was still upset! I knew that wasn't right, but the reason I was upset was that I was doing everything I could to help him. I felt that he had no idea what my family was going through to help him. Those were my feelings at the time, but I had to press through them and see them from his standpoint. My dad couldn't control himself mentally.

On the way home from church, my thoughts were, *Shirkyria, you can't take things personal with your dad; it's not him.* God had to help me with that a lot because I had a tendency to get in my feelings when someone came at me the wrong way. However, even though things were a bit rocky with my dad at church. In all, I loved my dad, and I knew I couldn't stay mad at him for long.

One of the *great* moments that I love sharing is about the celebration we had for my dad's fifty-fourth birthday. I got him a birthday cupcake cake and cooked him his favorite meatloaf. I wanted his birthday to be special because I didn't know if it would be his last. On my way to the nursing home to pick him up, I was so excited to spend his special day with him. Little did he know, I had a big surprise just for him. I walked into my dad's room with a big smile and hug and said, "Happy Birthday, Daddy!", Sadly, he didn't remember, but it was my job to help him remember. While me and my dad were talking, in walked his surprise. It was his son—my baby brother. My dad's face lit up; he was so happy. My brother lives in Texas, so he hadn't seen dad in a while. My dad was excited, but my brother was being challenged at that very moment. My brother could tell that his dad was not the same man that he once knew. We had phone conversations about dad's memory declining, and I was keeping him updated on dad, but there is nothing like seeing it with your own eyes. My brother was in tears. I could tell that he was hurt. We left and went back to my house. I went into the kitchen to finish the last touches on the food, got things set up, and I gave my dad and brother some alone time since it had been a while since they had seen each other. Dad was having a great time. We ate, sung "Happy Birthday," and took pictures. Dad was happy, and it was a great day in the books for us!

I received a call from the administrator to inform me that after two months, the state had denied my dad's long-term Medicaid. When she told me the bad news, I was so confused and frustrated. I left work immediately and went straight to the nursing home to talk with the administrator face to face. When I arrived, I was shown the documentation by the state for the reason behind the denial. He was denied due to over-income! I got even more frustrated. I was like, *how?* The income he was receiving was under the income bracket for Medicaid, so I thought. It was then explained to me that the state was also counting my dad's social security disability that *he wasn't even receiving*—due to social security automatically pulling their overpayment. The state counted that as income. The administrator let me know that I had three options: 1) I could file for an appeal, 2) I would have to pay out of pocket, which would be $4,500 a month, or 3) move my dad out. She handed me a thirty-day eviction notice. My heart had been filled with fire at this point. As soon as I walked out of the administrator's office, I could see my dad walking back to his room. As bad as I wanted to say hello, I could not. I walked out of the nursing home and immediately called my lawyer. I explained to the lawyer the denial, and he informed me the next step would be to file an appeal; on the way home, I just cried and asked God for help. I did not understand why the state denied care for my dad. I felt the state's decision was wrong. I was trying to deal with the news but still execute the plan to appeal going forward.

We submitted the appeal, and all we could do from this point was wait, which was hard because my patience was delicate. The nursing home received notification of the appeal and had to put the eviction on hold. This also allowed me some time to brainstorm.

I felt like God was testing my patience because, again, I needed an answer now. I needed some peace of mind. Every day I would hope to receive a phone call of good news that the appeal was approved. When I didn't hear an answer by the end of the day, my anxiety levels went up, and my nerves got bad. A couple of weeks went by, and I finally got the phone call from the lawyer that the state had also denied the appeal. The first thing that came out of my mouth was *what* and *why*. The lawyer explained that my dad was denied again basically for the same reason, *over-income!* The state didn't budge. I felt like I had failed my dad. My stress level was closer to the edge. I didn't know what else to do. After the nursing home received notification of the second denial, they issued me another eviction notice. I was getting fed up.

I had set up a meeting with the lawyer and gave them a copy of the eviction notice. The lawyer continued to give me hope. I needed it because I knew that we had less than thirty days to fight the state's decision. Even though we were all frustrated with the state's decision, we decided to keep fighting. Keep in mind that during this time, we were still playing the waiting game on social security's decision on his disability. There were so many moving parts that I literally wanted to just pull my hair out! Let me tell you; God was the *only* one keeping me sane.

Time went on, and the lawyer and I were still fighting the state. We were trying to find the right people to talk to so that someone would hear our case. I was wrestling over the phone with different people daily, which started to drain me even more. As time went on, I just felt like I was hitting a brick wall. We weren't getting the answers that we needed. While dealing with this, I chose not to see my dad much during this time. It wasn't that I didn't want to see him; I missed my dad every day; I just didn't want him to see me upset and stressed. I felt like I had failed him, and I didn't want to face him at that time. It was complete chaos for a moment there.

As we got closer to the deadline, my husband and I started to prepare for my dad to live with us. We knew that we would have to adjust and make some space. Our kids had their own room, but we eventually had to sit down to explain that their paw-paw was moving in with us for a while. This meant that the boys had to share rooms. This caused us to rethink the space that we were in.

While we waited, my husband and I decided to look at some homes because we were living in a rental home at the time. We decided to visit a few open houses not too far from the home we were staying in. The homes were beautiful but high-priced. One day when we were out driving, we had noticed some new homes that were being built in the same neighborhood that we were living in. There were five open houses, and I remember this particular house that we looked at that gave me that "this is my house" feeling. As this thought came into my head, my husband and I said, "This is it," at the same time. At the time, we were skeptical of buying a house because being in the military requires you to be flexible and ready to move at any given time. The service lifestyle does not allow you to settle anywhere if you ask me. Although these thoughts were crossing our minds, the realtor saw how much we loved the house, and she started speaking a new language to us. She let us know instantly that we would pay an earnest payment of $2,500 to hold the house while going through the buying process. We told her that we would talk about it and get back to her. A couple of weeks passed, we got so busy with taking care of things for my dad that I overlooked the multiple emails from the realtor. She was checking to see if we were still interested in the house. She already understood that I was dealing with a lot with my dad. She told us that other people were interested in the house, but I could tell that she really wanted us to have it. It was like God was trying to give us this house. I felt that God was trying to get our attention through her because she came back and notified us that her manager had dropped the cost of the earnest payment to $500, which we were grateful for. Immediately we started the buying process; we were so excited! Listen, we drove by the house every day declaring that "this will be our new home." We stood on faith that God would bless our family with a brand new home. Although we had some hurdles to jump through, we walked by faith and not by sight (2 Corinthians 5:7). The buying process was quick, smooth, and right on time. When the day came for us to sign the closing documents, it was pure joy! It was all God that did that for us during the chaos that we were in. Not only did God bless us with a brand-new home, but the builder also gave us our earnest money back, paid for our closing costs, and paid one year of our house insurance! You are talking about a triple blessing. This was the *win* that we needed during a season of tribulation.

We packed up and moved into our new home, which had

more space that would be necessary for my father to move in with us. The old house did not provide enough space for another adult. We got his room situated also enhanced our security with cameras and a monitored system.

We were at two days left before the eviction. I still had hope that I would get some good news that my dad could stay in the nursing home. I didn't want to have to explain to my dad again why he had to move again. The thought of explaining things like this to him was stressful because I knew that he wouldn't understand, and it would just confuse him even more.

Finally, the day came where either I had to make a full payment out of pocket, or the state approved his Medicaid. If that didn't happen, I had to pick up my dad when I got off work. I was at work and struggled to focus. I kept checking my cell phone, hoping I would get a call from the lawyer or nursing home with good news. My nerves were so bad; my mind was plagued with worry. That afternoon I had received a disturbing phone call from the social worker at the nursing home. She told me to come and get my dad right away and that my dad knew that I was coming to get him, so he tried to get out the door. My dad had no idea that I was coming to get him. Somebody from the nursing home told him intentionally, knowing it would change his mood and he would become anxious. I informed my supervisor that I needed to leave immediately to get my dad, and I was *out of there*.

When I walked into the nursing home, I saw the social worker and my dad sitting at the front. She gives me this story that my dad knew I was coming to get him, he tried to run out, and they caught him and had to hold him because he was being combative. Her story just didn't sit right with me. I truly believe that someone from the staff told my dad that I was coming to pick him up to *purposely* set him off so that I could come to get him sooner. They were ready for my dad to leave, and they were willing to lie in order to make it happen. You have to understand that nursing homes have to keep bodies and beds to make money and Meaddill was no longer making them money. My dad was relieved to see me. I had to get my dad out of there. I was so upset about the way this was handled.

I packed up his clothes and some toiletries, and I told the social worker that I would be back another day to pick up the rest of his things.

The nursing home officially evicted my dad, and I still had no answer from the state. This left me no choice but to move my dad in with me and my family. This was another hard turn in this journey that you have to be mentally prepared for. You might be in a place where you are battling with the state or the nursing home. I encourage you to keep fighting but never run out of options. Be prepared at all times, especially when it affects your household. In the battle against the state, we lost; however, God blessing us with a new home at the right time gave us the option of moving him in with us, which was a *win*.

Chapter 6

Weary Days and Nights

My dad was on his way to live with me and my family. With that, I knew what I was getting my family into, but I didn't know how hard it was going to be for my family and me to adjust. I was so thankful for my husband's support in helping me with my dad. He took off from work to help me multiple times with no complaints! Him being in the military and his career field requiring deployments constantly took him away from our family. However, God worked it out for him to be home during this time.

I explained to my dad that he would be living with us for a while. When we arrived at our home, I showed him the room he would be sleeping in. Once we got him settled in, my husband and I helped my dad get dressed for bed. We had everything set up because we wanted to make sure that he was comfortable. As soon as he got in the bed, he told my husband and me, "Thank you." The sincerity in his eyes gave us a sense of relief. We did not know how things would play out now that he was in the house, but we knew that he wouldn't have to worry about feeling stressed or being abandoned.

The next day, I had informed my supervisor of the situation with my dad living with us. I had to ask for a few days off to get some things lined up for extra help. My supervisor was incredibly supportive, and that was a relief because I didn't want to lose my job; however, I was prepared just in case it did come to that. God had his hand over my job. He clearly showed me unconditional favor! There were times when issues came up, and I would have to leave work early to cater to my dad. Due to this happening often, I felt that my boss would get fed up and fire me, but God did not let that happen. God had my back!

The next couple of days, I spent time on the phone with DHS (Department of Human Services) to see what kind of help my dad could get while living with me. There were so many benefits that my dad was eligible for, such as medical equipment and meals. They informed me that it could take up to three weeks for a nurse to come out to evaluate him and set up the things he needed, which was disappointing because I needed help sooner than three weeks. I got a call the next day from an agency letting me know that a case manager and nurse would be out to my home the next day—*only God!* This was great news! Another prayer God answered. I prayed for God to provide me with access to an adult daycare that was close to my home, and He gave me just that. The daycare that we chose had hours that lined up with my work hours to where I dropped my dad off before work and picked him up after work. The adult daycare had good activities that helped keep my dad active. Another plus was that they were open on Saturdays! That was break time.

Not too long after getting things situated with the day-care, the nurse and caseworker came over to our home. They were asking questions about my dad to see what kind of assistance he needed. My dad needed all the assistance he could get. The nurse and caseworker were so helpful. They helped make this transition seamless. They cared about my dad, and that meant a lot to me. They delivered a month's worth of frozen meals a few days later, and it was helpful. As things were settling in, I reflected on my progress in lining up things for my dad. I could do nothing but shout, *"Halle-lujah!"* I was so grateful for all the help I had received at that point. God was pouring favor!

My husband received approval from his job to take off for two weeks to also assist in this transition. He had decided to take off to help my dad with the adjustment in our home. Now keep in mind that my husband had already taken at least a month off in the beginning in between the trips to Texas, meetings with the lawyer, and any other business. Due to my husband serving the military, his job is quite demanding, so it can be difficult for him to take leave. Although he could deploy at any time, God worked it out to where my husband could stay home to help me. I need to brag on my husband for a bit because everything that happened up to this point, which was *a lot*, could not have happened without him by my side. He was so supportive, and he never complained. He cared and loved my dad just as much as I did. When I felt down and stressed, he was there to pick me up and encourage me. When I was about to lose my mind many times, my husband was there for me. He did the things that I was not comfortable with at first, including showering, toileting, shaving, and so much more, until I got comfortable doing it.

As we continued to get settled in the new house, my dad was experiencing sundowning, meaning that his days and nights were mixed up. Many nights he would be restless, confused, irritated, and pacing. I can't tell you the type of stress this brought on me and my husband whenever he would get out of the bed, or we noticed any type of movement from the camera system. I would have to get up and remind him of what time it was and let him know that it wasn't time to get up yet. He would say "Okay" and get back in the bed, but most of the time, he would get right back up. He would take all of his clothes off and urinate on the carpet and window. Sometimes that would make me so mad because I knew that when he did that, he did it for attention. It was like my dad was becoming my child. You know when you have a newborn baby, and they are up every two to three hours. That is exactly how it was with my dad. My husband and I would be dragging out of bed to clean up the urine and change his clothes so that he would go back to sleep.

During the week, on the days that I went to work, I would get up an hour early to get my dad ready by helping him shower and get dressed. Once I got my dad dressed, he would eat breakfast and take his meds. After he was situated, I would proceed to help my kids get ready for school and myself ready for work. Before I would head to work, I would drop my daughter and dad off at daycare. It took me a while to adjust to this routine because my dad would wake up multiple times throughout the night. Not only that, I would have to wake up an hour early to get a head start on helping my dad shower and dress just to make sure we left the house on time. You can imagine how tired I would be, but after a while, I had it down like clockwork. I was overwhelmed, but God helped me.

Many people were concerned about my dad living in my home. They felt like it was not safe due to the possibility of him lashing out at me or his grandchildren. Department of Human Services could take my children if I allowed that to happen. As much as I wanted to believe that he would not lash out at me or the kids, I had to accept the reality that he wasn't in his right mind. I knew that if he did lash out, he would not realize what he was doing. Although it would not have happened intentionally, it still could have happened. At this point in time, my dad needed more care than what the caseworker was able to provide. This caused me to reach out to Adult Protective Services to see if I had any options since the state was denying care. In only a few months, my dad began to decline rapidly. I needed more help. Taking care of him created a heavy burden that I did not know how much I was able to take. It started to become clear to me that there would eventually be a time when taking care of him by myself was going to be too much.

I was able to get some guidance from the caseworker, but that was not all God had in store when I asked Him for help. One day, I got a call from one of my older cousins that called often to check on my dad and me. Every time she called, she would pray and encourage me. Word got back to her that my dad was staying with me. She did not think that it was safe to have my dad around the house with my children due to the changes in his behavior. She told me with urgency that I needed help and that I needed to write a letter to the President. While she was telling me this, I thought to myself; *It won't hurt to write the letter.* I knew that it was going to take some thought because it was much to ask for. I agreed to write the letter, and my cousin's instruction to me was once

I was finished with the letter, to call her so she could pray before I mailed it off.

Another cousin, which is one of my dad's nieces, was one who also called all the time. I thank God for her because she was always there when I needed to vent. She would always pray and encourage me to help me through my rough days. There was family that would message me on Facebook or text me from time to time to keep me uplifted. I was grateful for any support or encouragement because it was needed. At times I found myself pondering on the thoughts of how the family was going on with their lives every day and had no idea what my family was going through, *no idea!* Honestly, that would make me angry, but I could not allow that to get to me because being mad was pointless.

One Sunday, my daddy was not having a good day. I was already stressed, and I could see that my dad was on the couch upset. I could hear him talking negatively, and I immediately got upset. At that moment, I told him he should not be mad because I was doing my best. I broke down in tears trying to explain the best way for him to understand what was going on with social security and how I was fighting so hard for him. I knew that he would not understand the entire situation, but he needed to know. All the buildup frustration came out at once. I eventually stopped talking and went to my room. I was lying on my bed in tears because that is all I could do at the moment.

I could overhear my dad talking to my husband, saying, "Why didn't she tell me sooner?"

I heard a voice telling me to stop crying, get up and go talk to my dad and pray with him. I ignored it the first time. Then my husband comes into the room to tell me that my dad wanted to talk to me. I didn't want to at first because I needed some time alone. After I was able to contain my emotions, I went into the living room where my dad was, and I could tell in his eyes that he was hurt and clueless. I apologized for taking my frustrations out on him. I wanted him to know that I was doing my best to help him and didn't want to stress him. By the expression on his face, I knew that he felt that I was hurt. He repeatedly apologized, which I was not expecting an apology for; he was fighting a horrible disease. As I was talking to my dad, I ensured him that even though this was a tough battle, I had his back.

We had a father and daughter moment, and as we were talking, I just felt in spirit to get my Bible and read Romans 10:9, "If you declare that Jesus is Lord, and believed that God brought him back to life, you will be saved." I begin to pray, asking the Lord to save my dad; my dad repeated after me, giving his life to Christ. At that very moment, a sense of peace overcame my household, and I could tell by the sincerity that he believed with all this heart that he had just been saved. The Bible says in Romans 10:10, "That by believing, you receive God's approval, and by declaring your faith you are saved." I will never forget that moment as long as I live. I realized how God used me at that moment for His glory. God allowed that moment to happen for a reason.

I finally finished the letter to President Obama; it took four days. In the letter, I explained the situation and asked the President if it was possible to help my dad get into a memory care facility. I also asked what can be done to keep this from happening to other families in a similar situation, even though my dad's was a special circumstance. The fact was that my dad needed help, and I needed help, and everyone who was in a position to help said that there was nothing they could do. I called my cousin, and she prayed over the letter before I put it in the mail. Not long after I had sent the letter, my dad's behavior fluctuated more extremely; he became short-tempered and easily agitated more frequently. I was receiving frequent calls from the adult care, saying that he would become aggravated and upset. He would be fine until around 3:00 p.m. when he saw other people leaving. He would get anxious and try to take his shirt off. I was receiving calls from the daycare quite a bit regarding the changes in my dad's behavior. One day I got a call from the daycare that he was anxious and moody; he was also trying to take his clothes off. I left work to go get my dad because his anxiety was too much. We got in the car, and he could not sit still. I was trying to get him to calm down, but it wasn't happening. I looked over, and my dad was trying to pull the door handle *while I'm driving*! This was terrifying because I was driving, trying to calm him down, and keep him from trying to get out of a moving vehicle. Thank God we did make it home safely. I checked the mail and noticed that I had received a letter from social security regarding an overpayment on his Medicare. Due to the overpayment, they did stop his Medicare which he needed, especially for his medication. I was not ready for that news. Things were just starting to settle down a bit, and the next thing, I'm blind-sided with an overpayment from Medicare. My dad needed all the Medicare coverage he could get. Once again, stress was building up, and I wanted to explode, but what good does that do? I had to pull it together and keep pushing. This was not the time to fall apart.

I needed help fast. I called a doctor to explain his elevated anxiety and told him about his behavior at the daycare and trying to get out of a moving vehicle. As I was on the phone with the hospital, I saw my dad in the living room on the couch, rocking back and forth, messing with his clothes, and he could not be still. The doctor advised me to bring my dad to the emergency room. I did, but I was heartbroken and scared at the same time. We waited in the emergency room for a virtual meeting with the psych doctor. When the doctor finally came on the screen to talk to us, I told him about my dad's behavior and the incident that just happened. The psych doctor decided to admit my dad into the behavioral medicine facility to adjusted his meds and find a nursing home placement. The doctor said that at this stage of my dad's illness, he needed twenty-four-hour care. I knew I could not give him this level of care, and to top it off, we had tried placing him in a nursing home, but due to the vendor payment and no social security, we were unable to afford it. It was at this point that I knew I needed God to assist me up this slippery slope of the mountain because I could not get my footing.

I stayed with my dad at the hospital until they transferred him to the facility. It was late, so I knew that I would not be able to visit him until the next day. I was restless that night and could not sleep. So much was going through my mind. I was not sure of the next step; I didn't want my dad in the behavioral facility again, but what choice did I have? This was hard! But I knew that God was still with me to walk me through.

Chapter 7

Facing the End

After a couple of days of my dad being admitted into the behavioral medicine facility, I went to visit him, and he seemed fine but confused. His nurse let me know that they were adjusting his medications and that he would most likely be there until they could verify that the medications were doing what they were expected to do. There was a meeting with the doctor along with other staff members to tell me that it was not recommended for my dad to come back to our house. He needed twenty-four-hour care. They explained to me that he was also having violent visions of apparitions of people with guns trying to attack him, which caused his anxiety to increase. I explained the battles that we were facing with the state and how he couldn't move into a long-term care facility until he got approved for long-term Medicaid and social security to pay for the vendor payment. Even though I explained that to them, they were still willing to give it to try to see if a facility would still accept him under the current circumstances. I saw the sense of urgency with the staff. The social worker at the behavioral facility let me know that she would be making some calls. She kept me updated as she got feedback from her resources. As she fed me, I made calls to the lawyer and fed him information that I received as well.

Since they decided to keep my dad, I tried to visit with him every chance I got. The visiting hours were limited. When I did see him, my heart broke every time. I hated to see him in that place, but at that point, options were limited. I cannot even explain the way I was feeling. I was trying hard to keep myself together. My God, it was *hard!* Almost two weeks went by when I received a call from the social worker at the behavioral facility letting me know that the doctor thought my dad's medications were working and that his behavior was improving. She also let me know that there were two nursing homes that were willing to accept my dad. One in Enid, Oklahoma, and the other one in Tulsa, Oklahoma, and they were willing to accept my dad even with the circumstances until the state approved his Medicaid. Yes, I was grateful, but at the same time, I was hesitant because both nursing homes were a little more than two hours away. This was such a hard decision, but after some thought, I decided to admit him to the one in Enid. I spoke with the administrator at the nursing home in Enid. She sent me the paperwork that I needed to fill out. I informed her that I would not be able to move my dad's things during the week due to my work schedule. She gave me the okay for me to move his things on a weekend as I could inform the nurses of the situation. I informed the behavioral facility that I would be moving my dad's belongings and that the plan was to transport my dad to Enid within a few days.

As my family and I arrived at the nursing home in Enid, I was nervous. I knew that I didn't have any options, but I knew that God was opening doors, and I had to trust him. When we walked in, I was kind of relieved because I could tell that the nursing home was clean, and it didn't smell like urine. The nursing staff showed us his room, he did have to share a room, but the room was bigger than the last nursing home my dad was in. It took us a couple of hours to get his room situated. We had to make a few trips to the store. I was not leaving till I knew that he had everything he needed. I was in daughter mode, and I wanted my dad's side of the room to feel like home. I put his favorite recliner in there along with pictures to make it as comfortable as possible, and with all the relocating, I just wanted my dad to feel like he belonged there. After we were finished, I was hoping that this would be the last move. It was exhausting, and we were all tired. It had been a long day, and we were tired but still had to drive the two hours back home.

A few days later, the behavioral medicine facility transported my dad to the nursing home in Enid. I knew it would be an adjustment for him to be in a new environment seeing new faces. In a way, I felt guilty that I was abandoning him, and I was having doubts if I made the right decision. Many thoughts begin rushing like a raging river in my mind. *Should I have brought him back home with us? Should I have fought harder to find a closer nursing home?* I had to reassure myself that I had done everything within my power to find him a home. As I stated at the beginning, I visited almost every nursing home in the Oklahoma City area. I called many times throughout the day, every day checking on my dad. Not being close to him was stressful, and I always wondered if the staff was treating him right. Within that first week, I got a call from the administrator telling me that my dad was being combative. Not only was he being combative, but he was also physically touching the nurse's breast. With him being tall and strong, the staff started to feel uncomfortable around him. The administrator also told me that my dad was hanging out at the front desk and watching the nurses. As she was telling me this on the phone, I just shook my head. I didn't know how to respond, really. My dad would not allow the nurses to give him a shower. He physically threw one of the nurses and kicked her on the leg. The nurse and administration wanted to admit my dad into a psych hospital that was located in Ada, Oklahoma. She stated that there was a bed that came open, and the urgency in her voice let me know that he needed to go as soon as possible. She also let me know that this psych hospital in Ada, Oklahoma, was known to be good and that they sent patients there all the time. She was very confident that they would get him on the right medicine. This was such a hard decision to approve. I gave them the okay to proceed with the transport. I was so confused; he had just spent two weeks at the Behavioral medicine facility for medication adjustment. Was that all for nothing? I felt like I was torturing my dad; my back was against the wall.

The day came for them to transport my dad to the psych hospital. The nursing home stated that transport was taking place. I asked them to let me know when he leaves. I called a few times throughout the day while I was at work. Unfortunately, there was a delay with the transport services. I called the nursing home when I got home from work that day, and my dad was still waiting. I got off the phone, and I told my husband, "I will just drive to Enid and take him myself." Even though I was exhausted from work, I needed to act then because if my dad didn't show up, he could lose his bed because they only had one bed available that day. I called the nursing home back, informing them that I was on my way to the nursing home and that I would drive him to the psych hospital. It did cross my mind if taking him was risky due to his aggression, but this was a decision I needed to act fast on.

After a two-hour drive, we arrived at the nursing home shortly after sunset. We walked into the nursing home, and I immediately spotted my dad hanging around the front desk. He did not notice that we were at the front door until I said, "Hey, Daddy." I tried to explain to him that he was taking a ride with us. I went to his room to get clothes for him, and one of the nurses came into the room to have a conversation with me. By the look on her face, she felt for my dad; although she was one of the nurses, my dad hit her and left a bruise on her leg. She was not upset because she dealt with dementia patients all the time on a daily basis. All I could do was apologize to her.

It was approximately around 9:00 p.m. when we left the nursing home. We were so tired and had both worked that day. After we got everything my dad needed in the car, I proceeded to type the address into the navigation system to the psych hospital. To my surprise, it came up as a three-hour drive with all the urgency and everything moving so fast; I didn't realize how far Ada, Oklahoma was from the nursing home. I had to immediately take a deep breath, realizing that our arrival was going to be close to midnight. I made the call to the psych hospital to inform them that I would be bringing my dad instead of waiting on transport, and admissions said that they would save his bed.

My husband offered to drive to the facility so I could take a nap. After about two hours, I realized that my dad was not saying much. I could hear the kids sleeping, and when I turned around, my dad was asleep as well. My guess was that his night meds had kicked in, which probably kept him calm during the ride. I was kind of nervous with him being in one spot that long because I didn't know how he would act. I decided to stay up and keep my husband company and keep an eye on my dad as well. The ride was smooth and mostly quiet.

We finally arrived at the psych hospital a little after midnight. I knew that it was God that protected us to arrive safely. I called to tell them that we were parked out front. One member of the staff opened the door for us. I gave my dad love and said my goodbye. He was half asleep and didn't respond much. I watched as the nurse escorted him to the back. It was heartbreaking to see him leave. The administrator that was completing the admitting processes asked me a few questions and went over the paperwork. Besides the paperwork, he only needed a few pairs of his clothes. The facility provided the toiletries. I was informed that I would be updated on the status of his treatment and that visiting hours were Saturday and Sunday for two hours.

As we left, I just prayed to God to watch over my dad

and to make sure the staff was treating him right and hoping this was the last time his meds to be adjusted. I felt so much guilt and utterly helpless because he was being tossed around. I wanted my dad to be in one place and settled with great care. At the time, it was hard trying to find that. We did not leave the facility until around 2:00 a.m.; we were all tired. We arrived home around 4:00 a.m. and had to be up for work in two hours. Good thing the kids slept mostly the whole trip, so they were not too tired for school. I did not know how I was going to function on an eight-hour shift. I wanted to call into work so bad but, I had already taken so much time off. I was struggling to stay awake at work. God gave me strength, and so did coffee. My dad was on my mind heavily. When I took my first break at work, I decided to call and check on my dad. The nurse informed me that they started the adjustment on the medication and the doctor would be seeing him soon. However, I had enough faith to know that God was in control. It seemed like the first week that my dad was there, the days were slow. I updated the family if they wanted to visit him on visiting days. I was ready to see my daddy and anxious for visiting days. In that first week, there were a few incidents of him being combative and trying to fight the staff. It was going to take time for the new meds to work. The doctor added more medicine and increased some of the medicine he was already taking. I felt so bad for him—the worse feeling a daughter could feel. My dad was a strong man, and he was also tall, so I could just imagine the strength it took for the staff to control him. I am sure it took more than one person. Other than him being combative, he was still eating well and taking his medicine.

Visiting days finally came, and I was so excited to drive down to Ada to see my dad. When the nurse brought my dad to see me, I felt like a kid. He was smiling, alert, and he knew who we were, but sadly I noticed he had declined even more. Some conversations were one way because he did not understand some things I was asking him. We just kept talking and smiling. I was just grateful to see him. That moment took me back to when I was little and the times when I would visit my dad on the weekends. The excitement! I was always a daddy's girl. He was happy to see his grandkids, he did not say their names, but he knew who they were just by hearing their voices. Our visit came to an end after two hours. Once the aid took my dad back, I had a brief conversation with his nurse. She updated me on his progress, and she gave me a copy of his medication list that the doctor added.

I called a few times a day throughout the week to check on him; sometimes, he would be good, and other times, he would get triggered and become agitated. I didn't visit my dad for a couple of weekends to give other family members a chance to spend time with him. I knew that would make my dad happy at the time.

After about two or three weeks in the facility, the doctor believed the medications were doing well, and he approved to discharge and transport him back to the nursing home in Enid.

Things had seemed to be going fine in the first few days of him back at the nursing home until I received a disturbing phone call from the director of administration of my dad being combative. It was not good. His behavior was getting worse and worse. We thought the medications were working. She broke it to me that they would need to send him back to Ada, Oklahoma, *again!* In order for the doctor to get it right with his meds. Not only that, but she also told me that they were not willing to take my dad back due to his behavior and the safety of their employees and other residents. Excuse me, what? *Ugh!* This felt like a scary rollercoaster that was going in circles. My dad had not been at this nursing home long at all. All the time we spent driving there and setting things up in his room felt like a waste. However, I understood where she was coming from. She had to protect her employees. I could not argue with that. The psych facility in Ada had to find his placement in a facility that could really care for him.

Yes, you guessed it! My emotions were high. I cried out

to God, telling him how I didn't understand. What do I need to do? I needed direction. Approximately the next day, I received a phone call from the psych facility needing me to fax the paperwork over for me to fill out *ASAP*. I went to my supervisor, informing her of the situation, and she gave me the okay for the facility to fax the paperwork to my job fax machine. I was grateful for that favor because I knew that my job needed me to be on the phone working due to high demand. My supervisor and her boss understood the urgency of me getting this paperwork back to them. They knew what was going on from the beginning, so they didn't hesitate. That took off some relief.

The transport service picked up my dad from the nursing home and took him to Ada. I called the administrator at the nursing home to work out a day and time to pack his things. In my heart, I knew that God saw everything that was going on, and even though I felt I was not getting a clear direction, I knew that God did not leave me. Close friends and family were praying and encouraging me to keep my head up. Honestly, my faith was wavering; I did worry a lot, which is normal; I'm human. Even though my faith was not firm, I knew that God brought us too far and that He will never leave my side. His Word says in Hebrews 13:5, " I will never leave you nor forsake you," which always gave me some relief and comfort.

I had to keep fighting; I could not give up. I needed to talk to social security again and explain the urgency. Since my dad moved to Oklahoma, I had been talking to the person that had been assigned to my dad's application which was at the location close to my home. It was so hard to get in touch with her. Ninety percent of the time, I would get her voicemail, and when she did call, there would not be an update. I decided that I needed to take off a day to talk to her face to face. I called and was able to get an appointment. I was protected under FMLA. The lawyer was sending the appeals to the social security office in Maryland because that's where we were receiving the denial letters from. As we were conversating, she understood how fed up I was with social security, but this was out of her job scope. She didn't make the decision to deny his social security; it was out of her scope of what she could do. I am here to tell you there is always hope. The worker from the social security office told me to go a few windows down and talk to this certain person that handles waivers for overpayment. I didn't need to make another appointment, which worked out in my favor. I explained the situation that the lawyer and I had been battling with my dad's social security. As I was explaining everything from the beginning, I knew it was a lot of information to take in. The person I was speaking with informed me to fill out the request for waiver of overpayment recovery or change in repayment rate. I was also told to explain in detail to the best of my ability what happened. Remember, my dad received notification of overpayment a few years before he was diagnosed with dementia. So, I had to explain on the form that I didn't know why my dad did not report his income correctly. I have no answer for that. He was incapacitated. As I was filling out the form, I thought, why didn't anyone tell us to fill this out before? We were fighting for months with social security! For example, one of the questions on the form asked how much can be contributed to the overpayment. I put $50 down. Social security was already taking the full amount. I was willing to just pay $50 towards the overpayment so the vendor payment can go towards whatever nursing home he will be going to next. I was told that I would be notified by mail of the final decision. I still had hope that social security would show some mercy. All I could do from this point is put it in God's hands and pray for a miracle.

A little over a month passed, and my dad was still in the psych facility; the doctor adjusted his meds several times. During this time, I had not visited my dad in a while. I called every day, though. So much was happening all at once, and I really needed time to recoup. My body was giving me signals that rest was needed.

In other great news, my dad's son graduated from high

school; I was a proud sister. That was some news we all needed to hear at the moment. I knew daddy would have attended the graduation if he could.

I decided to take a trip to visit my dad. When the nurse brought my dad out, he was in a wheelchair, and it took everything in me not to cry in front of him. He was so sedated from all the medication that he couldn't even walk. I cannot even explain the pain I felt at that moment. I knew that he was declining more and more; he looked so different. He had lost more weight and was overdue for a shave. I asked the nurse why my dad had not been shaved, and the nurse stated that he would not let them. He was very combative when they would try. As I looked at my dad, he just sat in the wheelchair with his head down. I just stared at him for a while with such heartbreak. I did not know what to think. I just started talking, even though he was not responding. I just looked at him. He did not even recognize my voice, my husband's, or his grandkids'. He was out of it and barely awake. We did not even stay the full two hours, maybe forty-five minutes at the most. I could not take seeing him like that for another minute. I cut the visitation short. I got in the car, and it all came out. I cried like a baby, oh I cried! Why was this happening to my daddy? I need my daddy back! I hated seeing him suffer.

Going back a few years while we were stationed in Utah, a year after giving birth to my daughter, I was having a lot of pelvic pains. My doctor at the time couldn't tell me what was causing the pain. They did several tests, but the test came back normal. It was off and on. When we lived in Japan, I would have these same pains, and my doctor in Japan could not find anything. During this time, the pelvic pains were coming back but more consistent. Something was wrong; this was going on too long. I figured the stress I was under was a trigger. I made an appointment to see the doctor on base in Oklahoma and made the urgency for them to do more tests. I was not having pelvic pains for nothing. My doctor decided to go ahead and schedule an ultrasound. A few hours after the ultrasound, the doctor called me to tell me that my uterus had enlarged, and there were also multiple fibroid cysts growing on my uterus. The good news was that the cysts were not cancerous. We finally figured out where the pain was coming from. My doctor referred me to an OB/GYN doctor, and it boiled down to me needing surgery. The doctor explained that the procedure would be a partial hysterectomy. This meant that she would remove my uterus and cervix by abdominal incisions. The good news was that I was able to keep my ovaries. Even though I had dealt with pelvic pain for years, that was a hard decision to make because that meant that there would be no chance of having more kids. My husband and I came to terms with that. We were grateful for God blessing us with the three children that we have now.

I was also informed that the recovery time would take up to six weeks, and I could not drive for a week. Six weeks seemed way too long. I was hesitant because I needed to be ready to go when my dad needed me. Deep down in my heart, I felt that his surgery needed to happen. I had to put myself first this time. I had informed my boss of me needing to take another leave of absence pertaining to my health. I thought to myself my job was probably saying, *We have never had an employee take so much leave of absence.* Every leave of absence I needed to take, God poured his favor on me so that I would not lose my job. With that being said, my medical leave was approved.

By the grace of God, the surgery went well. No complications. The doctor reminded me to take it easy so that I could heal properly. I was in pain, but I was thankful for the pain meds to help with the relief. Even though I could not visit my dad on the weekend, I still called to check in on him. While on medical leave, I really used this time to rest. I slept *a lot!* I did not realize how tired my body was. My body desperately needed a reset.

Two months had gone by, and he was still in the psych

hospital. The doctor had to readjust his meds multiple times. It took a lot longer than we expected. I was not surprised when I would receive phone calls from family members on how my dad looked so sedated when they visited him.

While I was on medical leave, I received a letter. This letter was the miracle that I had been waiting for so long! It was the letter from the social security office saying that my dad's social security was *approved!* Do you hear me? *Approved!* The letter stated that my dad would receive his social security payment minus $50, which would go towards the overpayment. You are talking about a huge mountain moved! That alone was an answered prayer from God. Words could not describe how thankful I was.

Let me catch you up on what was going on at home. My husband was assigned for training for one month at the Air Force base in Wichita Falls, Texas. The base was less than two hours away, so some days the kids and I would drive there to spend some time with him. After my husband finished the course, a ceremony was held in which family was allowed to attend. On the day of the ceremony, I received an unfamiliar phone call. I did not hear my phone ring, but I noticed I had gotten a voicemail. It was a lady calling me from the social security regional office in Dallas, Texas. The message on my voicemail was her letting me know that she received notification of the letter I had written to President Obama and that she also read the letter. She wanted to know the status of my dad's care and proceeded to take some real action to get the state involved. Listen, when I heard that voicemail, I was humbled and in disbelief at the same time. Not only did the President read my letter, but he also took action by contacting the right people that had the authority to make things move. You cannot tell me God is not real. Prayer works! I realized that God had put this on my cousin's heart to tell me to write that letter, and even though I did not want to do it, I am so glad that I did. When God tells us to do something, we must be obedient, even when we do not understand the instructions. I do not take any credit; all glory belongs to Him. After the ceremony, I returned her call, and she told me that she also read my letter and wanted to know where things stood at the moment for my dad. I let her know that social security recently approved the waiver for my dad to receive his social security minus $50. She was happy about that. I also let her know that his Medicare was still not active. She made some calls, and within two weeks, my dad's Medicare was reactivated. Two of the huge mountains that I was facing were knocked over so that I could continue climbing.

The doctor decided that my dad's medications were adjusted enough to discharge him—perfect timing! A social worker from the psych hospital facility was searching for nursing home placement for my dad. Now I was able to pay the vendor payment to the nursing home. The next step was to apply for Medicaid long-term care. I contacted the DHS worker to start the application process. Shortly after, I received good news from the social worker that a nursing home located in Medford, Oklahoma, was willing to take my dad, considering his combativeness. The director from the nursing home in Medford reached out to me and sent me the admission paperwork.

In the beginning, the lawyer did all the paperwork for the first nursing home he went to, but I felt like at this point, the lawyer had given up. Not me! I decided to do the paperwork on my own. To be honest, it was not hard to fill out. I thought to myself, *How could I have done the paperwork myself instead of my lawyer?* But it was a lesson learned. The DHS worker that was over my dad's case informed me that it could take up to thirty days to process, but in the meantime, my dad would be under pending Medicaid. I was praying that the state would not deny him for the third time.

The nursing home in Enid still had my dad's belongings; I just did not have much time to drive to Enid and pick up his things while trying to recover from surgery. I called and spoke with the administrator in Enid to discuss my dad's things, and I was informed that they put his things in a storage area and were willing to deliver his things to the new nursing facility. I thought that it was very nice for them to do that. However, when it came time for them to deliver, they delivered his recliner, clothes, and wall décor, but they forgot his pull-ups and his TV. It seems the TV was not in the same pile as his other things. I was not really tripping on the TV because, at that point, my dad did not watch TV anymore. If he had his bed and recliner by the time he arrived, that was good enough for me. Do not get it twisted; I did drive down to Enid to get the rest of my dad's things. They were not about to keep my dad's TV, *lol.* Not on my watch!

Things were lining up with my dad's living situation. The psych hospital discharged my dad, and he safely arrived at the nursing home in Medford Praise God. I was so relieved that he was out of that psych hospital, and I never wanted him to go back.

Another phone call for the win; I got a call from the DHS worker that his long-term Medicaid was approved. This time *not* denied! However, the state would not cover him until the following month due to one of the assets being transferred, which was the car that was bought for my dad in a part of his spend down place. I decided I'd transfer the car to my brother as a graduation gift from dad. However, because

I transferred the vehicle, the DHS worker said it would be a one-month delay on coverage, meaning I would have to pay out of pocket. His social security disability would cover some of it, but not all. It was too late to transfer it back to my dad's name. So, I decided to drive to Medford and have a one-on-one conversation with the administrator. I was so nervous because I did not know what the solution would be. As I got closer to the nursing home, I was like, man; this nursing home is out in the country. I mean, it was in a small town. The outside and inside of the nursing home looked old, which I did not care about. My biggest concern was the care. A nursing home can be a five-star luxury, and the care be crappy.

When I first met the director person of the nursing home, she was very pleasant. I first thanked her so much for welcoming my dad. She ensured me that he was in good care. The nurses were well trained in handling Alzheimer's patients. She expressed the care and love the staff showed to the patients, which gave me comfort. At that moment, I felt that I would not have to move my dad again. I started to explain to her the situation of the transferred asset and how the state would not cover my dad until the next month and that his social security was not enough to cover it all. I explained to her, in summary, the past battles with the state and social security. She got wind of *all of it!* The look on her face was astonishing. What came out of her mouth in response I was not expecting—I will never forget. She looked me in my eyes and genuinely said, "Don't even worry about it, just pay his social security vendor payment and don't worry about the rest. We will start brand new next month." When I tell you that I was not expecting that response, it blew me away. I wanted to cry. I just gave her a hug. That was another miracle from God. Nursing homes are a business like any other business. They need money to keep things running. However, money was not the concern on that day.

After talking to the director, I went into my dad's room to check on him; he did have a roommate. However, it felt good to see him in a new place and not have to worry about moving him again. I knew that he would experience some confusion in a new area. I went into daughter mode by spending time fixing up his side of the room with familiar photos.

This season was rough, but God lined things up right on time. Yes, I was stressed with the nursing home in Enid kicking him out, but God had things under control. My dad's Medicaid was approved, social security approved, Medicare was reinstated, and he was safe while receiving twenty-four-hour nursing care. Praise God! When things seem to turn for the worse, know that God is still moving behind the scenes. He reminded me many times that I did not have to fight my battles alone. He fought them for me! He put people in place to help me.

I updated family members once my dad got settled in Medford, so they could come to visit him whenever they chose to. As for me, my medical leave had expired, and I was well enough to go back to work. Even though it had expired, I was still on intermittent FMLA due to the care for my father.

During the week, I would take two, maybe three days and leave work early or wait till I get off of work to drive to the nursing home to visit with my dad. It got tiring after a while driving two hours there and back home. I felt that I needed to spend as much time as I could with him. He had declined so much in the last few months. Some days I would feel this heaviness in my heart to go visit my dad. Even if I had just seen him the day before, I felt a need to go right away. I remember one Saturday I had not planned on going to the nursing home. I was going to stay home and rest, but when I woke up, I felt in my spirit that I needed to go see my dad. I said to my husband I needed to visit my dad to-day. My husband would say, "Let's go." So, my husband, the kids, and I were on the road. Now my husband was just a couple of weeks away from leaving for deployment. Do you see how God worked that out with the deployment? He worked it out so that my husband could stay here to support me because he knew that I would need him. Once things got settled with my dad, my husband was called to go on deployment. God line things up for a reason. My husband wanted to see my dad before he left anyway. When we arrived at the nursing home, my dad wasn't in his room. We proceeded to walk around the nursing home to look for him, and a couple of minutes after we saw two of the nurses just walking with him and laughing with him, but what threw me off was me hearing my dad singing and preaching. Now, I remember when I could call and check on my dad, some of the care staff would ask me if my dad was a preacher; I was like not that I am aware of. Also, family that would call the nursing home would also tell me that they were being told about my dad singing. Everyone would get so tickled. So, when I actually saw and heard my dad preaching and singing about Jesus, I was saying to myself, *This is what the staff was talking about.* He looked so good; they had him shaved real nice and clean. When I said, "Hey Daddy," he didn't recognize that I was standing in front of him. He just kept singing and preaching—*hahahahaha.* One thing that did cross my mind was, *Is God giving me a sign that my dad is about to leave?* I was not ready for God to take him; he just got settled. My family and I walked with him and took him outside in the back sitting area. We talked, laughed, took pictures. I even took him for a walk, just me and my daddy—a very special moment.

Not long after that visit, my husband left for a five-month deployment tour. Deployments are always hard, but we were used to it. I knew he would hold it down, and he knew that I would hold things down at home. With my husband being gone, it causes adjustments to my schedule, so I did not drive to the nursing home during the week. I went straight home after work, but the kids and I would go on a Saturday or a Sunday to visit. Some of the family were coming from Texas to visit with him as well; they noticed how much he had declined and was coming to Oklahoma even more to see him.

I started to receive calls from my dad's nurse informing me of his lack of balance; he was falling suddenly. It raised concerns, and the nurse recommended physical therapy. I was so worried. They transferred him to a different nursing facility that offered physical therapy, and the great thing was the facility was only ten-fifteen minutes from my home, which was great. Since the facility was close, I was able to poke my head in many times. I was not fond of this facility at all; I saw the lack of care for their patients. It did not smell clean. A few days after him being there that he fell and hit his head which led to him getting stitches; I almost lost it on the staff. He didn't have a concussion or anything, just stitches, and the nurse staff decided to put a helmet on his head, so if he did fall, he would not hit his head. Well, let us just say my dad did not like having that helmet on. When I would see him try to take it off, I would remind him of the importance of keeping it on. It was nice to have my dad close, but there was really no progress with therapy. It wasn't doing any good. It was worth a try. The nursing home in Medford let me know on the day they were going to pick my dad and bring him back. I left work early so I could see him before he left. I arrived just in time, they were loading him in the back seat, and he was just smiling. I will never forget the moment before he left; I said, "I love you, Daddy," and he responded, "I love you too." The driver was in awe. Even though it's tough not having a full conversation with him, to hear him say "I love you" was enough for me.

Approximately four months passed, and my dad continued to decline; he was talking less, eating less, and still falling.

One day I went to visit, and as I walked into my dad's room, there were two care staff members. One minute my dad was okay, and the next minute, he had frozen up and stopped responding. The nurses were calling his name, and with no response, one of them said to me, "Say something to your dad, and maybe if he hears your voice, he will snap out of it." And that's exactly what happened. I said, "Hey, Daddy," and he responded. It was scary for a moment, but we were so relieved that he responded. The reality set in that my dad was not going to get better as parts of his brain were shutting down.

There was a time when I felt a pull to start preparing and look for funeral homes. I tried to ignore those thoughts, but I sensed that God was telling me to prepare now. This was hard to think about, but the more I ignored it, the stronger I felt it in my spirit. I had already decided to have him buried in his hometown, but I needed to find a funeral home that would do the embalming before they transport him to Texas. With Medford being a small town, there were only one or two funeral homes. I called one of them, and the receptionist was very helpful. She connected me with the owner, who was also helpful and answered all my questions. The owner said how much it helps to have funeral arrangements done ahead of time. When I did receive the paperwork from the funeral home, I honestly didn't want to fill them out. It was so hard to look at, but as hard as it was, I felt that it needed to be done. This will be one of the hardest decisions you will ever have to make for your loved one, but remember that you are strong, and you can push through it. Believe that God will give you the strength to press through.

Chapter 8

The Call

A little while after sending the paperwork back to the funeral home, the care staff requested a meeting with me about his care plan. Basically, it came to my dad needing hospice care. When I think of hospice, I immediately think of death, but it does not have to be thought of that way. Hospice provided more care. I have heard of people only needing hospice for maybe six months and improving well to not needing it anymore. This time I had a better understanding of how Alzheimer's disease breaks down your body—I was seeing it. The only way my dad would get off hospice was God's full healing. Yes, I believe that God is a healer. I wanted God to heal my dad, but we must understand it is what His will is, not ours. I updated the family about my dad going to be on hospice. They knew that this was the time to spend as much time with him as they could. I really liked the hospice care team. I was always notified before and after they would be with him.

The nursing home staff noticed family from Texas was coming just about every weekend to visit with him, and out of the kindness of the director's heart, the director approved to move my dad into his own room so the family would have more space to visit with him.

My dad's eating had really decreased; he was having trouble swallowing. The care staff had to pureed his food, basically blend his food together like baby food so it would be much easier to for him to swallow. If he didn't eat that, then they would give him a shake, which most of the time he would drink. As long as he had something to eat, I felt better.

The day came, my husband arrived home from deployment. Welcome homes are always nice. It was so good to have him home. We have been through many deployments, but this deployment was the toughest between working full time, taking care of my dad's business, driving back and forth to Medford, the kids, handling our household. After my husband got settled at home for a couple of weeks, we made a trip to visit my dad. When we walked into my dad's room, he was in his recliner with his eyes open and quiet. While talking to him, my dad then started singing, joking, and laughing. We just laughed and laughed. He would just sing about Jesus. I sensed that God's peace was over him, and I believe that he was also seeing angles because while he was singing, he would be looking up at the ceiling. I felt that my dad's time on earth was winding down.

Not realizing that this was the last time I would hear him

sing because shortly after that visit, my dad went into a really deep sleep for hours and completely stopped responding. When I would call to check on him, the care staff would let me know that he would wake up for a short period of time but would go back to sleep. He was bedridden at this point; he had no mobility. Hospice was coming more, and they would give him bed baths and make him as comfortable as possible. With him being bedridden, the care staff must turn him in every two hours so he wouldn't get bed sores. There were a few times the mean daughter side came out of me with the care staff when I would find out they were not turning my dad, because according to Hospice, he had some bed sores. I was not a happy daughter, and when they saw how upset it made me, pretty quickly, things got better with making sure he was turned every two hours.

One Saturday, I and some of the family from Texas were visiting my dad at the same time. We were just sitting there talking and watching my dad, hoping he would wake up. We knew he could hear us because when we would say his name and talk to him, we could see his tongue moving. It was like if he was in a coma. Hospice came in at one time to check on him, and the hospice nurse checked his vitals; they looked good. We were all there for hours, and he didn't wake up. During that week, I decided to visit him one day after work; when I walked in, my dad was in his chair, with his eyes open, but he was not talking. I asked the nurse aide if he had eaten, and she said he did not eat much, he had a food tray from dinner in his room, but the aide was afraid to feed him because she was afraid he would choke. I told her I would try. I started talking to him, letting him know that I was there and going to feed him. Even though he was not responding, I knew he recognized my voice. His dinner was mashed up soft like baby food. The first three bites, he was eating and swallowing just fine. That next bite, which was mash potatoes, he did not swallow it; next thing he coughed so hard, and mash potatoes were on my face, *hahaha*, it was time to put the plate down. I sat with him for a little while longer, wishing I could stay the night with him, but it was getting late, and I had to be at work the next morning. A few days later, I received a call from one of my dad's brothers; he was letting me know that he and his wife were at the nursing home, and my dad was up, and he was talking! I was so glad to hear that. I had missed hearing his voice so much. Hearing that news from my uncle made my day.

A couple of days after, I received a call from the nursing home that my dad had declined to the point that hospice needed to come to the nursing home *ASAP*. The hospice nurse called me and said that my dad was out of it again, where he was in a deep sleep, not responding, but his vitals were good, and they would come back to see him the next day.

THE CALL

Around 3:00, my phone ranged, and I see it's from the nursing home. In my mind, I was thinking they are giving me an update on maybe he woke up. As soon as I answer the phone, the nurse's exact words said, "Mrs. Gray, I'm sorry to tell you that your dad has passed." When she said that, I cried so loud in complete shock! My husband heard my cry and jumped out of bed, and by the look on my face, he knew that my dad was gone. The nurse asked if someone was there with me, and I told her my husband was. She asked to speak with him. My husband gave the nurse the information on the funeral home in Medford to call but not to pick him up till we get there. I just grab my head in disbelief; it felt like the breath was sucked out of me. My dad's battle with Alzheimer's ended. I knew I needed to call the family; I said to myself, *I don't want to make these calls,* but my husband reminded me that I needed to be strong. Riding in the car on our way to the nursing home, I was in complete silence; the news I had just received had not clicked yet. I didn't want to believe that my dad was gone. I was in denial.

We walked into the nursing home, and she told us to take all the time we needed, and she will call the funeral home. As soon as I walked into my dad's room and saw him lying on the bed face up, mouth open, I just broke down! I felt so weak. My husband was right behind, so when he saw me break down, he caught me from hitting the floor. I cried,

cried, cried! Pleading with God to please give me strength, *please give me strength!* I looked over at my dad again, and even though I could see his body, I knew his spirit was gone. His body was just the shell; there was no life. It took a while for my husband to get me to settle down. The pain I felt at that moment was unbearable. I was in disbelief, saying to myself, *My daddy is gone; he is really gone.* I really wanted to be by his side and hold his hand when he took his last breath. I was not ready to face this at all. My daddy was not coming back.

The funeral came to take my dad's body. I just stared in silence as they were loading his body in the van. As we were leaving, the nursing home care staff and residents gave us hugs and condolences. They expressed how much they loved my dad and saying how they will miss his smile, laughter, singing, jokes. The care staff stated my dad was their favorite. It felt good to hear that.

The two-hour drive back home, all I could think was the list of things I needed to do for the funeral. I was emotional and overwhelmed. It was so much to take in. I informed my job regarding my dad's passing, and they gave me some time off.

I already had a place in mind where I wanted the funeral to take place in Texas, but then I received some information on another funeral home that was owned by people within our family in Texas. We set up a time for me to come to Texas to complete the funeral details. On the other hand, after two days of my dad's passing was my birthday. I really wasn't in the mood to celebrate. My family was trying to cheer me to get me to celebrate, but I couldn't.

I received a phone call that day from the funeral home in Medford, Oklahoma, letting me know that they were done embalming my dad and were ready to transport him to Texas. I gave them the information on the funeral home in Texas. Then it came to me why God was having me get things lined up beforehand because he knew how I was going to react emotionally and the amount of stress handling the funeral arrangements. God always sees ahead.

A couple of days later, we made a trip to Texas for the funeral home arrangements. My dad's body had already arrived the day. Going over the details and picking out the casket and other things was nerve reckoning. I was trying to look strong on the outside but was so broken on the inside. Knowing the owners of the funeral home were family made things smoother for me. They wanted to take as much stress off of me as possible.

After all the arrangements were made, I went on an outing with my mom, aunt, and granny. It was much needed; they were really trying to lift my spirits up and just care for me. We went shopping and bought dresswear for the funeral. My daddy liked the gold color. I remember this gold suit he had worn to my high school graduation; *ah,* he knew he was clean. He loved that suit. My dad's sister and I went to a clothing store that sold men's suits, and she helped me pick out and bought his suit. Family love and support were much needed, and that helped me keep it together.

We drove back to Oklahoma the next day so that I could start working on the obituary and pictures for his tombstone. Between the pictures that I had and from family, my husband and I were able to create a tribute video to play at the funeral.

Two of our cousins on my dad's side are pastors, which helped me because they both agreed to help with the eulogy. Family that I had not communicated with in years was so supportive! It didn't matter if I didn't talk to them before my dad's passing. What mattered was us coming together and being there for one another during this difficult time. My dad was so loved, he was the best friend, dad, and many would say the favorite uncle. Family was taking it hard by his death.

We headed back to Texas two days before the funeral, and to my surprise, my one and only sister flew from California to support me. This brought a huge smile to my face. My sister is my best friend! She canceled plans to the Bahamas and flew to Texas. My sister wanted to lift my spirits to keep my mind off the funeral and took me to this place called Top Golf, and even though I am not a golfer, it was fun just to hit the balls. We laughed and ate good food—just what I needed. That night my sister took me to a comedy club. The main comedian was Benji Brown, now I have never heard of him, but he was so funny. I laughed so hard he had me in tears. It had been a long time since I laughed like that.

The funeral home let me know that I could come and view my dad's body before the viewing. I wasn't sure how I was going to handle viewing my dad's body, but I had to do it. My husband, my mom, my sister, and my granny came with me for support. Right before I walked into the funeral home, I can feel my stomach was just turning in knots. My mom saw the look on my face, and she said, you must be strong. I felt so weak. I walked into the funeral home, and the guy at the front desk pointed which room my dad's body was at. As soon as I saw my dad's picture on the wall, right before I walked into the room where his body was, I broke down. I could not contain myself. I kept saying, "I can't do this! I can't do this!" I can hear my granny saying, "It's okay, Shirkyria," and I can also hear my sister saying, "Shirkyria, he looks good! Come see him!" My husband was hugging me so tight, trying to comfort me and calm me down. When I was finally able to calm down, I proceeded to walk into the room nervously. As I looked at my dad in the casket, tears were just flowing; my heart was shattered. It hit me that this was not a dream; my daddy was not coming back.

My dad's side of the family is huge, and the funeral home saw how much family and friends were coming to the viewing. The owner was so nice to move us to a bigger chapel so the family would have enough room to sit. I was grateful for this. I only stayed at the viewing for a couple of hours. I was really tired and needed to mentally prepare myself for the funeral. I didn't sleep well throughout the night. The funeral was all that I could think of. I was not ready to say goodbye.

I tried to keep myself together while getting ready for the funeral. The service was going smoothly until there was a hiccup with the video tribute, the sound was low, and the video kept cutting in and out. Other than that, my dad's home-going was beautiful; he would have been pleased. When it came time for the opening of the casket at the end of service, I could feel my stomach turning knots. I realized this was my final goodbye; I just stood at the casket, tears flowing, not wanting to let him go. My husband was standing with me by the casket, and I hear another voice from a family member saying, "Shirkyria, you have to let him go." I didn't want to let him go. After the burial at the cemetery, we headed to my dad's hometown church, where food was set up for the family. There was a lot of food and family. It was good to see family that I haven't seen in years. On the other hand, I was mentally exhausted and still trying to process everything. On our way back to Oklahoma, we made a pit stop at the cemetery. As I stood over where he was buried, I was still in disbelief. I wanted to hear my dad's voice so bad. I needed God to help me face the death of my father.

Chapter 9

Death Wasn't It

I initially thought that I would go through the grieving process when I lost my father, but I had no idea how hard it would hit me. Although I knew he is with Jesus, it would take me time to become stable again. Now it was time for me to deal with who I was. I felt that I lost my soul. I felt I had lost my identity. I was dealing with so much between the loss of my dad, taking care of any business left for my dad, and family battles. It was too much to handle. My husband couldn't help me. My kids couldn't help me. My family couldn't help me. I couldn't help myself. I was deemed dead inside. I didn't want to do anything but sleep my life away. I would wake up in the morning and just stare at the ceiling feeling numb and in denial. It had only been three weeks since my dad had passed. On my first day back to work, I was dragging. I didn't want to talk to anyone. Of course, I received a lot of love and condolences from co-workers, which I appreciated. I remember logging on to my work computer, and my dad's pictures popped up, and I immediately broke into tears. I went to the bathroom to bring myself together, but it was so hard to do. Even though I felt numb when I was around people, I would put on this fake happy mask that I was okay so that people wouldn't ask me questions. I could tell that some people knew that I was putting on this fake smile. There were family and friends checking on me, and I would receive calls from a chapel that was through the hospice team that took care of my dad, and he would tell me that grieving was normal and it will take time for me to heal.

A month and a half later landed on Father's Day weekend. We were already in Texas visiting family for that weekend. On Father's Day, I woke up early with sadness in my heart; I couldn't call him to wish him a happy Father's Day. I decided to get dressed and drove to the cemetery. All I could do was cry. I missed him so much; I wanted to hear his voice and see his smile. My heart was broken; I wanted my daddy back. I was driving to Texas more frequently on the weekends just to go to the cemetery, and every time I would go, I would just cry and cry. I would be so emotional when leaving the cemetery. My grieving was becoming unbearable to handle. I decided it was best to resign from my job; I could not focus, and I was mentally in a dark place.

My little cousin on my mom's side came to Oklahoma during the summer break for two weeks. One day while we were at the mall and I was getting ready to pay for my item when I received a text picture of my dad's tombstone. I was lost for words for a moment; on the other hand, I was like, *wow,* it was breathtaking, and I was very pleased. I called the funeral home, expressing how much I loved the tombstone. It looked exactly how I wanted, and I knew that if my dad could see it, he would be pleased.

Our family reunion was coming up on my dad's side. I was on the fence if I wanted to go or not, and some of the family really wanted me and my brother to come. They thought it would be good for us. I thought it would be good to be around family, and my kids getting to meet family they had never met before. We would represent our dad. My husband was on Temporary Duty (TDY) in another state, so he was unable to attend. On the day of the family reunion, I went to pick up my brother, and we stopped at the cemetery beforehand. It was a moment for me and my brother. We both cried with so much hurt and pain. Our father was gone. We were his only two children. With him being gone, he would have wanted us to stick together and look out for one another. We both went through ups and downs with our dad; what parent doesn't? I knew without a doubt that me being the big sister, he would have wanted me to look after him. I was going to do just that. When we arrived at the family reunion, there was so much family and food. We were taking pictures laughing and having a good time. When it came time for the family to line up to make their plates, my eyes immediately started watering. In my mind, I pictured my dad in line laughing and cracking jokes, ready to eat some good food. I was trying hard to hold back the tears, but they came out. It gets to a point when the mask comes off, and people see the hurt in your tears. I couldn't hide the pain at the moment. It felt different not having our dad at his family reunion.

I was sinking into a very dark place, a deep depression. I was watching the tribute video over and over every day. I tried to hide my depression from my kids so they wouldn't see the pain on my face. I was falling apart; I felt like I could not move forward with my life without my dad. I felt such heavy guilt like a part of me believed that if I have done more, maybe my dad would still be alive. I started to blame myself for his death. I found myself wanting to commit suicide. I found myself wanting to give up on life after time. I cried and pleaded to God, but that was not working for me; at least that's what I thought.

One day I was at home changing the sheets on my bed, and as I was looking for a pillowcase, I happened to see the pillowcase with a picture of me, my dad, brother, and both of my sons. It was a picture we had taken at a retreat when he visited us in Utah. Why did I have to see that? Looking at the pillowcase just put me over the edge, darkness was all over me. I was drowning mentally; then I heard in my mind, "If you kill yourself, then you can be with your dad." My emotions were all over the place. I was having repeatedly suicidal thoughts and thinking how I didn't want to live anymore. I was emotionally a mess, and grief had a stronghold on me. I texted my husband and told him I loved him. I got my husband's gun out of the safe, and as I held the gun, I kept hearing, "Do it! You won't feel like this anymore." Deep down, I knew that if I had pulled that trigger and took my life, there would be no coming back; my husband, my kids, and other family and friends would be hurt. So many thoughts were going through my mind. There were already bullets in the gun; all I had to do was pull the trigger. Satan, who is a deceitful liar and whose mission is to steal, kill and destroy, was trying to take me out. Even though I knew he is a liar, I felt like I had no life in me. I was stuck in complete darkness. As I was sitting on my bed, still holding the gun, trying to decide if I should end it all, my phone started to ring. I saw the call was from a friend of mine that I pray with, so I quickly put the gun back in the safe and answered the phone. My friend had no idea that I was in the moment of thinking about taking my own life. God intervened for her to call at the right time. I knew that had to make the devil mad. My friend knew that I was still hurting from the loss of my dad, so she would call to check on me a lot. We talked for a couple of hours, and she prayed. I needed God to restore me and heal my broken heart. I did not want to feel this pain anymore; it was too much to handle. My husband comes home, and he sees that I was emotionally unstable. I could tell that his heart broke for me; he wanted to help me but didn't know how. I told my husband that I needed to be admitted into a psych hospital that would get me on depression meds. This was a hard pill for my husband to swallow, but as he always does, he supported me. He wanted me to get the help that I needed so I would feel better. Though it was hard, I called the psychiatric hospital in Ada, Oklahoma. I told them about my depression, and they let me know that there was a bed available. This was the same psych that I had to put my dad in. This early during the day, our kids were in school, so my husband had time to drop me off in Ada and make it back home before the kids got out of school. I told him not to tell the kids where I was and to only tell a few people that I was close to where I was. When we arrived at the hospital, I remember texting my mom and my granny, giving them a brief message of me getting help, and they would not be able to reach me on my phone for a while.

This time we were not here for my dad; we were here for me. I never thought I would see this place again. My husband by my side stayed with me until after the admission process, and then he had to leave. I did not want to leave my family, but they could not help me. I had hit rock bottom. The care staff showed me the room that I would be sleeping in and explained to me the rules. I was also told that I had to attend the group therapy sessions, and if I didn't, then it could delay my release. My first night was uncomfortable. I was sleeping in an unfamiliar area. There were many people with mental health problems. The nurse gave me depression meds. The next day I was not in the mood to eat breakfast, so I just sat at a table by myself till our time was up. After breakfast was our first group therapy session. We had to go around the room and introduce ourselves and tell why we were there. Overall, the session was okay. All I could think about was calling my family. I was missing my husband and my kids. I didn't know how to talk to God at this point. I felt so lost. We could not have our cell phones; I had my husband take mine home. I could only use the hospital phones, which only had two available and only two hours of phone time. There were three group sessions throughout the day; I didn't want to talk to anyone. I chose to participate so that I could go home sooner. I also had a private session with the social worker, and I felt that I could open to her, so I shared the grief I was dealing with due to the death of my father, which was causing my depression. The session went well; she understood my grief.

I chose not to eat lunch and dinner. I just sat at the table by myself again, quiet till our eating time was up. After thirty minutes of taking my night meds, it made me sleepy, so

I couldn't stay up late. I had a roommate, and she was nice. She was dealing with mental illness and had been there for three weeks. She was ready to go home. I could not sleep well; I would wake up several times throughout the night. We slept on mats that were not comfortable. This made me more depressed, but what kept me going was hearing my husband, kids, mom, and siblings' voices. They let me know how much they loved me and encouraging me to get better. At lunchtime on the second day, the nurse aide noticed that I was still not eating. He walked over to me, and we had a heart-to-heart conversation. He was encouraging me to eat something because he has to document if I don't eat or how much I did eat. He also explained to me that if I did not eat, it could delay my release. I agreed to eat. I basically had to force myself to eat at least half of my food. The food was not that good. On the third day in one of our group sessions, we had to say what progress have we noticed that was made. For me, I noticed that I had not cried in two days about my dad. I guess the medicine was kicking in my system. I was starting to feel a little better. The social worker came over to talk to me after one of the group sessions about her getting reports of my progress, which according to her, was better. I told her that I was ready to go home. I was only there a few days, but this was no place for me. The social worker explained that at the end of the week, the doctor, she, and some of the care staff will have a meeting with each individual and, depending on the reports, will determine if the doctor would release me.

The day came for the meeting with the doctor. I was a bit anxious. If the doctor didn't release me, then I would have had to stay another week. I walked into the room and saw the doctor, a few of the care staff, and the social worker. When I saw the doctor, I thought I said to myself, *This is the doctor that kept adjusting my dad's meds.* He had spent so much time with my dad's case. He asked me how I felt; I told him good. He briefly went over my depression and the meds he prescribed me, and the progress notes from others. I shared with him what led to my depression and suicidal thoughts. When I said my dad's name and told them I was his daughter, I noticed how their facial expression changed. They knew my dad very well and remembered that I was the one that was caring and making all the decisions for him. The doctor recommended me to keep taking the depression meds for a short period of time. He said grief is normal, and the depression will get better. He discharged me to go home the next day. Some people were discharged along with me, and others had to stay another week. It was sad to know the different mental illnesses that people were battling. I called my husband and told him that the doctor released me to go home the next day. He was so happy, and so was I.

When my husband picked me up the next morning, he arrived with some beautiful red roses and a card with a big smile. I was smiling from ear to ear. We hugged each other so tight. In the first few minutes of walking outside, I was thankful; I never wanted to be in a psychiatric hospital again. It felt good to be outside. A week was too long, and just to think my dad was in this place three-four times for weeks. I could tell by my husband's face was a sigh of relief and joy; he told me how much it hurt him to see me in that place. I felt like I needed to. My husband didn't tell the kids that I was coming home. I wanted to surprise them; I had missed them so much. The kids thought I was taking care of business, but I knew once I saw them, I needed to tell them where I was and why.

After a few weeks of being on the medication, I was feeling a little better but still dealing with grief. I felt like the medicine was causing me not to have any emotion. I felt numb, like a walking zombie. I just wasn't myself; I wanted to be in the dark and just sleep. I had no interest in doing the things I used to do. Our close friends came over one day just to talk and catch up. They knew I was dealing with grief, but they had no idea I was at a psych hospital. As we were talking, I decided to share what was going on with me. The first thing my friend said was, "I knew I should have called that day." What she meant was the day I was attempting to commit suicide, she said that I was on her mind while she was at the grocery store, then she said on her way home I came to her mind again. I have learned when God puts someone in your spirit, we need to either call them or pray for them. She did not know that I had a gun in my hand, but she sensed something was wrong. She said, "Shirkyria, there would have been a lot of hurt people if you had taken your life."

I was approved twelve sessions with a grief counselor. Family thought it would be good for me. I really didn't want to talk to a stranger about my grief, but I decided to make an effort and at least try. The sessions were an hour, and sometimes we would go over. The counselor was compassionate and allowed me to release the different emotions I was dealing with. I was sad, angry, guilty, depressed, and in denial. The lessons she was teaching me in ways of not allowing grief to take control over my life. She told me, just like others, that I did all that I could do for my dad. There was nothing else that I could have done. I could not stop God's will from taking him. I may sound selfish, but my dad's passing was hard to accept. He was a part of me, and I was a part of him. I was so glad my dad gave his life to Christ before his mind declined to the point where he could not understand how to give his life to Christ. I know that my dad is no longer suffering; he is rejoicing in heaven with Jesus. A part of me wanted to go with him, and I could not. It was a daily fight with depression. I was trying to come out of depression by going to counseling and doing things to lift me up, and the more I tried to come out, the harder I had to fight. Not only were the medications making me feel numb, I noticed other changes in my body. I was having hand tremors, trouble sleeping, mood changes, and fatigue. Not only that, my anxiety was high especially driving at night. All of a sudden, I was so nervous driving over bridges, which was so weird to me. I'm thinking, *What is really going on with me?* I decided to visit my primary doctor for a checkup. I shared with my primary doctor the depression, anxiety, hand tremors, and lack of sleep I was battling with. She ran some blood tests, and the next day I received a call from the nurse stating based on my blood results, my thyroids were unbalanced, and my doctor decided to refer me to an endocrinologist. I didn't have much knowledge of how thyroids worked, but from what the nurse was saying, my thyroids needed to be checked right away.

Not long after receiving the news regarding my blood results, I had my first visit with the endocrinologist. He educated me on how the thyroid functions in your body, which releases specific hormones that travel through our bodies and help regulate our breathing, moods, blood pressure, body temperatures, and metabolism, and having an imbalanced thyroid level can negatively affect your bodily functions. He felt that my thyroid gland was enlarged. The medical assistant took some blood and scheduled a follow-up with my results. A couple of days after my appointment, I received a call regarding my blood results. She explained to me that my thyroid levels were high, and the doctor needed to see me. When it came time for me to see the endocrinologist, he said I had hyperthyroidism which was basically my body was making more thyroid hormones than needed. He medically diagnosed me with Graves' disease. This was another mountain in front of me that wasn't expected. Anxiety, mood changes, and fatigue are some of the symptoms of it. To my understanding, there is no main cause for this disease, but based on the research I have done, I believe that the amount of stress I had to endure as a caregiver messed with my thyroid functions. The endocrinologist further explains to me that treatment will consist of either medication, radiation, or surgery as a last resort. He told me that one out of three people goes into remission, and starting with the medication can take weeks in effect.

I was seeing the endocrinologist every three to four weeks. The medication was working well because my thyroid levels were functioning better. I could tell my moods were better, and fewer hand tremors. Of course, medications have side effects, and the one side effect that was devastating was my hair falling out. I was so upset and discouraged I almost gave up and wanted my beautician to cut my hair short.

She encouraged me not to cut my hair and to give it some time for my hair to grow back. I did not understand why I was still going through so much. I wanted God to give me some peace. I couldn't take anything else. However, I knew that going through this; God would bring me through it. I wasn't going through all this for anything. God was using this situation for me to testify for his glory. Satan wanted me to believe that God had left me. Even though things were rocky with my mental and physical health, I never stopped having faith in God. I knew that he was bringing me through the storm, and this mountain will too move. If you are a caregiver for your mom, dad, sister, brother, grandmother, grandfather, or any other family member, it is crucial that you take care of yourself. When your caregiver journey has ended, know that it will take time to heal for healing. Do not be so hard on yourself. You've done all you could do for your loved one. Take some time to get you back together, and do not allow grief and depression to take over your life. God knows your heart needs healing and will mend your broken heart. "He heals the brokenhearted and binds up their wounds" (Psalm 34:18).

Chapter 10

Putting the Mountain Behind Me

I was at home when my husband called me from work and recommended that I call the Alzheimer's Association that is located in Oklahoma City to see about volunteer opportunities. I was hesitant at first, but I decided to call, and the volunteer coordinator there asked if I could come in for an interview. The interview went very well. I shared with her my journey as a caregiver. The staff was so friendly and welcoming. The atmosphere felt like all smiles and love. I opened myself to be an assistant to whatever they needed help with. I was trained to help with donations, deposits, putting together binders for presentations, help with the annual Walk to End Alzheimer's. I was asked to do an interview with KFOR news to do a dementia virtual tour. During the segment, the family outreach coordinator gave me instructions to put on goggles that impaired my vision and earphones to muffle noise to get an idea of what it's like to have reduced functionality. The news reporter and I discussed the virtual tour after I was done, which made me realize what my dad was going through with his disease. I was nervous during the interview, but in the end, it went well. The news aired the interview on TV, and when my dad's picture came on the screen, my heart just dropped; I was like, *wow,* all smiles. I received so many calls and messages from family telling me how good I did, and my dad would have been so proud. God put me in place to share my story. A couple of months later, I received a phone call from one of my dad's friends that I had not talked to since the funeral and told me that she saw the interview on a global network! I was in wow. God gets the glory because He moved to make that interview spread wide.

Volunteering at the Alzheimer's Association really helped with my grief because I have always enjoyed volunteering and helping people that needed assistance. I attended my first Alzheimer's Walk; it was a very successful event. Hundreds of people walked. It was so amazing to be a part of it. I came to really enjoy helping at the Alzheimer's Association; the staff there feels like family. I love them so much. I am now a facilitator for caregiver support groups through the Alzheimer's Association. It is very heartbreaking to hear other caregivers' stories about their loved ones that have dementia and also what they are going through being full-time caregivers. It is a blessing when I am able to share my own life experience in the support group and helpful tips that helped me get through many of those trials and tribulations.

God has also blessed me with the opportunity to help caregivers by giving me the idea to start a non-profit organization S.Y.G (Sending You Gifts Through Thoughts Of Love), and the mission is uplifting and supporting caregivers. Me and my team create caregiver baskets with aromatherapy products, gift cards, coffee mugs, journals, and other things to uplift and support caregivers.' I want caregivers to know that they are not alone and to remind them of the importance of self-care. We are currently working on organizing caregivers' luncheons, family functions such as movie nights and picnics. The big event that I am so excited about is hosting an annual caregiver's retreat at a nice resort where caregivers can come for a relaxed weekend and connect with other caregivers. The first one will be in Oklahoma, and I believe moving forward, we will have the retreats in other states. God has done so much already with S.Y.G, and I truly believe that He is going to do so much more than I can even imagine. My desire for S.Y.G is to honor God by being a blessing to caregivers and share my testimony. Caregivers, God is right there with open arms, ready to help, and He loves you. He sees all that you are doing to care for your loved one; He sees the battles and the tears.

Another testimony I would like to share is I had applied for a receptionist position at an assisted living facility about five minutes from my home, and although I did not get that position, God opened up a door for them to hire me to help build a new program that was put together by the sales director. The sales director who interviewed me for the position and I clicked instantly! I could tell that she was so passionate about the program and the residents. We shared each other's; testimonies and the goodness of God. It was a heartfelt interview. I fell in love with this program because I could relate to it. I remember how nervous I was moving my dad to the memory care facility. As a caregiver, you want to make sure your loved one is in a facility that will take care of their needs. The program was designed to more attention to new residents in their first few months there to ensure their transition moving into the facility was smooth. For example, when a new resident has signed their contract to move in, it was my job to make sure that things were set up, such as welcome baskets, welcome folders with laundry schedule, housekeeping schedule, and food menu. These things had to be together before the resident moved in. I would spend one on one time, whether it was eating lunch or doing an activity with them, just to get to know them better. I understood the anxiety and stress with moving your loved one to a facility, so the goal was to help make the new resident feel welcome in their new home and putting the families at ease, so they feel that they have made the best decision. Do you see how God lined that up? I was grateful for the opportunity

God had given me to serve the residents and their families. God has also blessed me to be accepted into The University of Oklahoma, pursuing my Bachelor's in Social Work. I am currently a junior, and I believe in my heart this is what God wants me to do. If it's God's will for me, my desire is to continue my education with a master's and doctorate degree in Social Work. The enemy has been trying so hard to stop me from finishing school, but he can't stop me. I am doing God's work to help His people. My vision is to build a memory care facility that will be an excellent service to families and their loved ones. This memory care will honor God. I already have a name for it. I can't even explain the ideas God has given me for this facility. I don't know the location, but God has given me confirmation that it will come to pass. The Lord says in Habakkuk 2:2-3,

> Write the vision and make it plain on tablets, that
> he may run who reads it. For the vision is yet for
> an appointed time; But at the end it will speak,
> and it will not lie. Though it tarries, wait for it;
> Because it will surely come, It will not tarry.

I am excited to see what God is going to do.

As you have read, I had a lot of mountains in my way. Mountains looked at me as I looked at them for three years, but through it all, *God!* Yes! You can say it too—*But God!*

God allowed me to go through those things not only to increase my faith but to make me stronger. Yes, there were many times when my faith wavered, and I wanted to throw in the towel, but what God taught me was you have to be firm in your faith. Your faith moves mountains. You can command that mountain to get out of your way by activating your faith. Jesus says in Mark 11:23 says, "For assuredly, I say to you, whoever says to this mountain, Be removed and be cast into the sea and does not doubt in his heart, but believe that those things he says will be done, he will have whatever he says." Matthew 17:20 also says that if you have faith as small as a mustard seed, you can say to this mountain; "Move from here to there and it will be moved. Nothing will be impossible for you!" Our faith is in God. Have faith that God can move mountains that are obstacles in your life.

Social security, nursing homes, and the state told me *no* over and over and over, and even though those were the biggest mountains to move, I did not give up. I had to keep my faith activated to move the mountains out of my way. Caregivers, if you are faced with some of the same challenges, speak to that mountain boldly with God's Word and command that mountain to move. Don't give up! Don't give up! Don't allow mountains to defeat you! You are stronger than you think, and you will get through this. When you feel like the weight of the world is on you, and you are the only one caring for your loved one with no family helping you, remember that God is right there with open arms. Don't stay angry with family members that do not help you care for your loved one; forgive them and give them to God. Give all your worries to God, trust, and watch Him move.

Alzheimer's is an awful disease. I encourage you to cherish the memories you have with your loved ones while they are living. Hold on to those precious memories you share with them. When you feel like you want to explode, go to a room and take a deep breath, pray and just cry out to God for help—He will rescue you.

Caregivers, please take care of your health; self-care is so crucial. You must take care of yourself; because your loved one depends on you; they need you more than you ever know. Your loved one may say or do things that upset you, but keep in mind that it's the disease. As hard as it may be, don't take it personally. If your loved one has passed from Alzheimer's or any other disease, know that you will get through grief and allow God to heal your broken heart. Fight through depression. Don't allow it to have a stronghold on you. Be strong and try to do things that give you joy. Now I am not a preacher, and I am still learning in my daily walk with God.

If you don't know Jesus or believe that He is real, I am

here to tell you that He is very real! He is our Savior and Father, and He loves us very much. He deeply cares about your concerns. Everything He does is for His glory. I don't take credit for anything. All glory belongs to Him, and if it was not for God being with me, I would not have made it. God saved me from taking my own life, and He will save you too. Listen, you don't have to go through this alone. Give your life to Jesus right now! Romans 10:9 says, "If you declare with your mouth, Jesus is Lord and believe in your heart that God raised him from the dead, you will be saved." Cry out and tell God the battles you are facing and how you need Him. I'm not saying the battles will go away. What I'm saying is that God will give you the strength and grace to get through the storm. Don't tell God how big your problems are. Tell your problems how big your God is.

God used me to give my dad the opportunity to give his life to Him, and now I know without a doubt that my dad is in heaven; he is no longer suffering. Yes, I still have my moments when I cry; I miss my daddy every single day. He was a big part of my life for over thirty years. I will always hold on to the memories we shared. I will see my daddy again when it's time. You will have to make some really tough decisions, and people may try to tell you that it's not the right decision and give you their two cents. You may fall a lot, but God is there to pick you back up. Stand firm and know that you are doing your best because, at the end of the day, you are making sure that your loved one is getting the care that's needed. When your caregiving journey has come to an end, please don't beat yourself up; remember that you did all that you could do, and you fought with your loved one to the end. Be encouraged. Thank you for allowing me to share my testimony with you. God bless.

Letter: I Miss You, Daddy

It has been almost four years since you have been gone, and not a day goes by that I don't think of you. There have been many times I want to pick up the phone and call you just to hear you say, "Hey, Yonta." You were the only one that called me by my middle name—hahaha. I miss seeing your beautiful smile, laughter, and hearing your funny jokes. The day you left this earth, my heart shattered, and I felt a void. I did not know how I could move on without you; it seemed impossible. I did not want to let you go, but I knew I had to, and I knew you would want me to. You were the best dad a daughter could have, and I will always be grateful to God for allowing me to know you for thirty years. One of the best days that I can recall is the day I saw you get saved by accepting Christ as your Lord and Savior; this has given me much peace and a resolve to see the same for my friends, family, and others. We all miss you so much. I always carry you in my heart and uphold the lessons you've taught me. I know you would be proud of me, and knowing that pushes me to face the mountains and elevate.

I will always love you, Daddy,

Your daughter,

Shirkyria

Bibliography

God's Word. God's Word to the Nations Bible Society, 1995.

About The Author

Shirkyria Gray is from Dallas, Texas, and is a military wife of seventeen years and a mother of three beautiful children. She is currently pursuing her bachelor's degree in Social Work through the University Of Oklahoma. Shirkyria is the founder and CEO of S.Y.G INC. (Sending You Gifts Through Thoughts Of Love), which is a non-profit organization dedicated to creating thoughtful gift baskets and services for family caregivers. God put it on Shirkyria's s heart to write about her experiences as a caregiver for her father to encourage and uplift the millions of other caregivers that are going through the same trials and tribulations. It is her desire to build a strong support community for people helping people.